Transnational
Monopoly Capitalism

Transnational Monopoly Capitalism

Keith Cowling
Professor of Economics, University of Warwick

and

Roger Sugden
Lecturer in Economics, University of Edinburgh

WHEATSHEAF BOOKS · SUSSEX

ST. MARTIN'S PRESS · NEW YORK

First published in Great Britain in 1987 by
WHEATSHEAF BOOKS LTD
A MEMBER OF THE HARVESTER PRESS PUBLISHING GROUP
Publisher: John Spiers
16 Ship Street, Brighton, Sussex
and in the USA by
ST. MARTIN'S PRESS, INC.
175 Fifth Avenue, New York, NY 10010

British Library Cataloguing in Publication Data
Cowling, Keith
    Transnational monopoly capitalism.
    1. Economic development   2. Capitalism
    3. Monopolies
    I. Title   II. Sugden, Roger
    338.8'2   HD82

    ISBN 0–7450–0191–2
    ISBN 0–7450–0267–6 Pbk

Library of Congress Cataloging-in-Publication Data
Cowling, Keith.
    Transnational monopoly capitalism.

    Bibliography: p.
    Includes index.
    1. International business enterprises.   2. Capitalism.
    3. Monopolies.   4. International division of labor.
    5. Income distribution.   I. Sugden, Roger.   II. Title.
    HD2755.5.C68   1987   338.8'8   87–4965
    ISBN 0–312–00954–2

Typeset in 11pt Monophoto Times by
Latimer Trend & Company Ltd, Plymouth

Printed in Great Britain by
Billing & Sons Ltd, Worcester.

Contents

Preface

This book has grown out of Keith Cowling's earlier book *Monopoly Capitalism*. Roger Sugden, in his doctoral research at Warwick, pursued further the impact of transnational corporations on both product and labour markets, and subsequently the authors decided to join forces and produce a book which focused on the themes of monopoly capitalism within a transnational world. Keith Cowling would like to acknowledge the stimulation and help provided by a long line of graduate students at Warwick who were interested in pursuing issues of monopoly capitalism. Both authors wish to thank Christos Pitelis for helpful discussion throughout, and Mark Casson, Steve Davies, Steve Dowrick and Paul Marginson for their helpful comments on parts of the book. Teresa Forysiak at Warwick and Chris Barton, Maureen Hay, Gloria Ketchin and Nicky Valente at Edinburgh did the typing. We are grateful to all of them.

Keith Cowling
University of Warwick
Coventry

Roger Sugden
University of Edinburgh
Edinburgh

1 Introduction

This book is about an economic system – the system which dominates the present world economy outside the centrally-planned economies. That system is dominated by giant economic organisations with a transnational base: the transnational corporations. Since they dominate the system we shall be closely concerned with their structure and behaviour, but we are not primarily concerned with developing a book which focuses on the detailed aspects of the transnational corporations – a quick browse through any university library will unearth a multitude of such volumes. Rather we are concerned with extending the analysis of monopoly capitalism by explicitly recognising the transnational base of its central actors. The line of analysis follows that of Kalecki (1971), Steindl (1952), Baran and Sweezy (1966), and Cowling (1982), not because these books have been central to the literature on the transnationals – indeed Kalecki, the originator of this line of analysis, is totally silent on the subject – but because they provide the building-blocks with which one can begin to construct an explanation of how an economic system can evolve under a capitalism which has reached the monopoly stage.[1] We are thus interested in the transnational corporation primarily from the perspective of its contribution or role in the evolution of the total system of which it is simply a part, albeit a powerful part. Since we are not proposing a text on the transnational, our construction and description of this essential part of our analysis will inevitably be simplified. Nevertheless, as we hope to demonstrate, as part of our purpose we shall seek to identify a rather different view of what exactly

1

constitutes the essence of the transnational than has been previously put forward. Indeed, we shall be offering a different view of the essence of the firm.

As well as being primarily about the evolution and present state of the economic system, rather than about the details of the transnationals, the book focuses primarily on the industrialised countries of the capitalist system, using Britain as a particular example, although an essential part of our task is to recognise the breakdown of the world dichotomy of advanced industrialised countries on the one hand, and backward primary producers on the other, with international trade between these groups dominating world trade. The evolution of the transnational corporation has progressively destroyed this simple dichotomy. In contrast to the earlier history of the development of monopolies and cartels around the turn of the century, when protectionism was demanded to restrict or eliminate foreign competition in domestic and colonial markets, the new period of international oligopoly is characterised by demands on the part of the giant corporations for free trade and the supra-national institutions to pursue and sanction it.[2] It is to this new imperialism of free trade orchestrated by the transnationals which this book is addressed.

The central focus of our analysis is on the consequences of the evolution of the monopoly capitalist system for the distribution of income and, in turn, the implications of such redistribution for the macroeconomy. We shall argue that the growth of transnationalism itself leads to monopolisation tendencies within such a system, which in turn imply a potential for a rising profit share, but the consequences of this for the level of aggregate expenditure will imply a secular stagnation tendency. We shall maintain that the advent and growth of the dominant transnationals has served both to sustain and augment such tendencies.

We shall also be concerned with deeper issues of democracy and the quality of life which we see as intimately connected with the issues of distribution and stagnation. The essential element of democracy is the ability to control one's own future and the future of the community. This will always be determined, to a significant degree, by access to material goods, which in turn is related to the ability to gain employment, and therefore income, for those without property. Freedom will always be conditional on the existence of an economic surplus, and in turn the quality and distribution of that freedom will be determined by its distribution. The quality of life we also see as being directly related to the overweening dominance of the giant corporations which, with the development of transnationalism, leads to the imposition of a world cultural homogeneity.

Most of the book will be concerned with determining the dramatic consequences of the present economic system. But we shall also begin to map out an alternative system which allows for the democratic determination of the distribution of income and the achievement of full employment; which sustains and enhances democracy by expanding our limited political democracy into the economic arena; and which protects and augments the cultural independence of national communities. All this will be based on the development of a community economic autonomy which is denied in a world of transnational dominance.

The book proceeds from this introductory chapter to a chapter dealing with the essence of the transnational corporation. The theory of the firm, and therefore of the transnational, is restructured around a definition of the firm which identifies its essence as a locus of strategic decision-making which results in the incorporation of market transactions within the ambit of firms. Thus we define a transnational corporation as a means of coordinating production from one centre of strategic decision-making when this coordination takes the firm across national boundaries. It is important to recognise that the boundaries of the firm are no longer defined in terms of ownership, but in terms of control over production, either directly or through the market, for example via subcontracting. Thus the extent of the transnational is not easily defined since it is no longer measured by the collection of international assets directly owned by that corporation, but should also incorporate those market transactions which are directly under its strategic control. Although raising empirical difficulties, we regard our definition as the only satisfactory starting-point for our exploration of the consequences of the growth of transnationalism. However, before proceeding with this task, Chapter 2 also raises the question of why transnationals are created in the first place. The arguments offered focus on product market domination, where the key to our analysis relates to the necessary, and yet somewhat paradoxical, coexistence of rivalry and collusion.

Having established the desire to dominate product markets as giving rise to the existence of the transnational organisation of production, we turn, in Chapter 3, to the effect of the evolution of transnationalism on product market domination. We argue that the development of a transnational system of production and trade by the giant corporation gives it an added dimension of power within any specific market. Not only can the threat of the diminution of such power as a result of uncontrolled international trade be averted, but also the potential for market share augmenting activity can be increased as a result of both increased capacity and extended product variety. Given that these accretions to market power are only readily available to the giants, the disparity in power between them and their smaller rivals is increased. Recalling our definition of the transnational firm, we can readily see that such augmentation of market domination can come through the control of international market exchange as well as via the extension of the assets of the firm across national boundaries. Noting that transnational corporations are of increasing importance, and that they imply increasing market domination, we conclude that market domination by a relatively few giant corporations is increasing. The last section traces through the implications of such monopolisation tendencies for the distribution of income.

Chapter 4 takes up the issue of labour market domination raised in Chapter 2, alongside that of product market domination development in Chapter 3, emphasising the fact that theories of monopoly capitalism relate to labour markets as well as to product markets. The first theme analyses the fundamental asymmetry between capital and labour: namely, capital can be organised internationally, but labour, in general, cannot. The second theme relates to the international division of labour which results from the existence of transnational corporations. The last theme of the chapter considers the consequences for the distribution of income between labour and capital of the growth of product market domination coupled with labour market domination in a world of transnationals. The growth in the potential share of profits in such a monopolising system cannot easily be reversed by worker resistance because of the difficulties of organising transnationally. As a result, a tendency for the share of wages to fall will emerge from such a system.

Chapter 5 extends the analysis by focusing on the impact of such a redistribution of income on the evolution of the macroeconomy. We present the basic argument of the monopoly capitalist literature that such a system will develop a tendency to secular stagnation because the resulting redistribution of income will tend to lead to a decline in the growth of aggregate demand. We also develop a supply-side argument for the emergence of stagnation within specific advanced industrial countries. This springs from the increase in the power and militancy of organised labour, associated with the evolution of the system, which, in turn, leads to an accelerating wage–price spiral. The consequence of this process is a tendency for capital to migrate from high-wage cost economies to other locations. We argue that the global processes of industrialisation and deindustrialisation orchestrated by the transnationals are socially inefficient and undemocratic. We also conclude that stagnation will be a more pressing issue within a world in which the transnational control of production and markets by the dominant firms within the system is increasing, not only because it will become more likely, but also because it will become more unmanageable. We are involved in a negative-sum global game which will continue until we see quite radical changes in the way the international economy is regulated.

Finally we make some suggestions on the construction of an alternative system. Rather than starting by listing the ways in which we need to begin to regulate the transnationals, we have chosen to set down what we see as the central elements of a democratic economic system which can be counterposed to the system of transnational monopoly capitalism we experience today. Of course, we are exaggerating the true situation. We have not experienced a 'pure' system of transnational monopoly capitalism: over the years many democratic elements have been incorporated into the structure. And yet if we take at face value the wish of democratic governments to eradicate the substantial inequalities within the countries over which they preside, and also to remove the often more glaring inequalities between countries, we can only wonder at the strength of the forces opposing such declared intentions. Of course, in many cases, the intention is more apparent than real, and in recent times we have seen leading politicians come to power with no such intentions. But if one were to suppose that most democratically elected governments in the post-World War II era had some, at least minimal, commitment to such egalitarian ideals then the continuing gross disparities in income and wealth are indeed a resounding affirmation of the powerful inegalitarian forces embedded within the existing economic system. Indeed, there is increasing evidence now of the dramatic growth of a new and much more overt inegalitarianism. It is only quite recently that the rich have been willing to state publicly that the obvious way out of the current crisis of unemployment would be the re-establishment of a great sector of personal service, where those 'productively employed' could take on those without work, with such expenses being, hopefully, tax deductible.[3]

As a prelude to our construction of an alternative democratic economic system we make the argument for the incompatibility of democracy with capitalism, and its growing incompatibility as the system of monopoly capitalism evolves. Combined with the argument for the essential compatibility of democracy and economic efficiency, we then have powerful justification for the introduction of a system of democratic economic planning. Lest mention of planning conjure up an image of a centralised, bureaucratic determination of all detailed aspects of economic life, nothing could be further from the system we have in mind.[4] Planning would introduce democracy into production and the market economy, and it would be strategic, selective and decentralised, dominating the market in its long-term strategic implications, but working through the market in its short-term operational detail. A combination of a demand-side strategy designed to maintain full employment and a supply-side strategy designed to shape the long-term industrial landscape will together provide the environment within which dynamic, relatively autonomous economies can evolve. The creation of this network of relatively autonomous communities will in turn provide the basis of a new internationalism based on cooperation among successful economies rather than competition based on fear which is the hallmark of the present order.

NOTES

1. The term 'monopoly capitalism' will be taken to include the quite general, perhaps ubiquitous, case where markets are dominated by a few corporations – what is often termed oligopoly.
2. With some significant exceptions; for example, the response to Japanese expansionism led to demands by European and American industrial interests for restrictions on Japanese imports. More recently we have seen an increasing accommodation to this expansion.
3. These suggestions were made in a speech by the Chief Executive of British Aerospace and picked up by Neil Ascherson in his column in the *Observer* (13 July1986), where he lamented the evolution of London into a neo-Edwardian society with its enormous gulf between the haves and the have nots.
4. It is of interest here to note the present demands within the Soviet Union for dramatic political change in order to secure economic dynamism. See *The Guardian*, 22 July 1986. They are basically arguing that greater democracy will be a spur to economic efficiency. Our demands for democratic change within the capitalist system are entirely complementary.

2 Theory of the Transnational Corporation

A sensible starting place for a discussion of transnationals in the world economy – and accordingly our concern in this chapter – is to consider what they are, and why they arise. This gives the discussion a solid foundation and will provide insights that can subsequently be built upon and explored in greater depth. Moreover, failure to begin an analysis on the right footing will lead it badly astray; if the aim is to explore a world dominated by transnationals we should have little or no success if we did not understand these basic issues. It would be like trying to explore an uncharted area of deepest Africa by starting in Latin America.

There is of course a vast literature on transnationals and so it should come as no surprise that definitions have been provided in the past. Indeed, there have been many. But the problem has been a tendency simply to give a definition without deriving it from first principles. This is all very well and undoubtedly has its place but is lacking in depth and therefore prone to error. What is needed, bearing in mind that transnationals are merely firms in some sense operating in at least two countries (see for instance Buckley and Casson, 1976) is a coherent definition well-founded in the theory of the firm.

This has been provided by authors working in the Coasian tradition. The starting-point for such analysis is the Coase (1937) paper, which argues that production is coordinated either by market exchange or within a firm; i.e. that the firm is *the* means of coordinating production *without* using market exchange.[1] As regards transnationals this analysis has been developed in particular by Buckley and Casson (1976); they simply see a transnational as a firm in which the coordination of production without using market exchange takes the firm across national boundaries.

This is clearly an analysis focusing upon market exchange. Indeed, following Tomlinson (1984), it could reasonably be said that the primary purpose of the Coasian framework is simply to analyse markets.[2] However, we reject this focus.[3] In doing so we are not alone. For example the market/non-market dichotomy has been criticised in the past by analyses that nevertheless accept the Coasian view confining the firm to non-market exchanges.[4] For instance, Imai and Itami (1984) talk of non-market exchange using 'market principles', whilst agreeing that market exchanges occur only between firms or between firms and consumers. See also Brown's (1984) discussion of firm-like behaviour in markets. But our analysis goes far beyond this. We challenge the Coasian view at a more fundamental level. Its concern is the *type* of exchange used in production – i.e. market versus non-market. Firms and transnationals are simply confined to the latter. Yet this ignores the important insight that the crucial factor is the essential qualities, the very *nature* of an exchange – regardless of whether or not the market is involved. Indeed, the type *per se* is of no interest; it should be some underlying quality which is the foundation for analysis because it can only be the essential characteristics which really distinguish exchanges, not superficial attributes. The key problem is therefore to determine the critical essential characteristics and to solve it we shall delve more deeply into the theory of the firm.

Hand in hand with these different analyses of what is meant by a transnational go alternative views on why they arise. This should not be unexpected because in each situation the subject matter differs. Unsurprisingly Coasian analysis – more commonly known as internalisation – maintains its concern with market versus non-market exchange.[5] Its method is to ask why there should be one rather than the other, the answer coming from a characterisation of the environment in which exchanges occur. Thus coordination of production via market exchange is seen as a benchmark, departures from which have to be explained. The only contemplated basis for a departure is the incentive provided by the possibility of at least some people gaining and nobody losing. This is a Pareto criterion, founded upon the view that anybody and everybody has some sort of veto over outcomes they find undesirable – in other words, the economy is made up of voluntary exchanges.

Add to this the notion that a complete set of perfectly competitive markets is Pareto-efficient and the Coasian framework is complete (although compare Dunning's view in his 'eclectic' theory).[6] If production was everywhere coordinated by market exchanges which were perfectly competitive, there could be no Pareto improvements. There could therefore be no non-market exchanges, because these will only arise if they are Pareto-efficient. There would therefore be no firms. So it follows that: firms, hence transnationals, arise from the incentives to bypass imperfect markets with non-market exchanges. The source of these incentives is in fact seen to be savings on transactions costs, a concept explored in detail more recently by the likes of Williamson (1975) in his analysis of markets versus hierarchies.[7] They provide the basis for the crucial efficiency implication, although the possibility of cost reductions when moving from market to non-market transactions is not itself sufficient to yield Pareto improvements. This is guaranteed by the voluntary exchange principle, a concept which can perhaps best be explained by a simple example. Suppose individuals A and B are engaged in interdependent activities within a firm. The argument typically runs: the fact that a firm exists implies that A and B are better off, or at least that neither is worse off, using a firm organisation rather than an external market, otherwise they would have chosen to use the external market. In other words, then, in moving from market to non-market exchange individuals A and B will be simply sharing out the savings on transactions costs.

In contrast, our focus in defining a transnational implies that we must seek an alternative framework for explaining their existence by moving away from an obsession with market versus non-market exchange, to explore the very nature of exchanges. Our analysis is in the spirit of Marglin's (1974; 1984) discussion of the transition from the putting-out system to the factory in the English textile industry. He focuses in detail on what is happening in production, in particular on control of the work process, and does not get diverted into the market/non-market distinction. Again, then, the type of exchange is superficial. What is important is what is really happening when firms arise. However we can happily parallel the Coasian method. Thus in examining a particular exchange within a firm, the critical issue is: why an exchange of this *nature* rather than *another*, market or non-market? Our answer calls for a fundamental analysis of firms' behaviour and, unlike the Coasian concern with a complete set of perfectly competitive markets as its starting-point, we shall begin with an oligopolistic environment. Moreover, because internalisation's efficiency implication is so important from a welfare standpoint, we must pursue whether or not it still holds.

WHAT ARE TRANSNATIONAL CORPORATIONS?

In looking for the distinctive feature bringing an exchange within a firm, rather than leaving it outside, particularly interesting has been the concern of a very extensive literature with decision-making. This is significant because analyses of decision-making tend to concentrate directly on what is actually happening when production takes place; they tend to go to the heart of production rather than concentrate on superficialities. This is precisely what we are looking for. In general this is seen in such seminal works as Simon (1959), where it is argued that satisficing behaviour is the norm, and Cyert and March (1963), who develop an analysis of decision-making closely associated with all behavioural theories of the firm.[8] More specifically – and for us more importantly – it is also seen in analyses of the control of the firm.[9]

Especially interesting here is Zeitlin's (1974) view that control implies the ability to determine broad corporate objectives despite resistance from others – in other words, to make decisions over such strategic issues as a firm's relationship with its rivals, nation-states and workers, its rate and direction of capital accumulation, its sources of raw materials, and its geographical orientation. These decisions are especially important because they are fundamental to the direction a firm takes. The power to make such decisions confers the power to determine the fundamental behaviour of the firm, its objectives and the way these objectives will be pursued (see Scott (1985)). This is not to say that the only decisions being taken within a firm are strategic. However, it is to say that any other decisions are subordinate; in this sense strategic decisions are the pinnacle of a hierarchical system of decision-making. They constrain the operational, day-to-day decisions taken by managers over such tactical issues as the choice of promotional activities and of a particular project from a subset of alternatives. Moreover they also constrain – as do the operational decisions – the choices made by workers concerning work intensity, etc. Consequently whereas all three types of decision determine what actually happens in production, the strategic decisions play a prime role because, by definition, they determine the direction of the firm (see Pitelis and Sugden, 1986).

Accordingly, the notion of a centre of strategic decision-making goes to the heart of the way in which production is carried out and provides a clear basis for defining a firm and hence a transnational.

Accepting the Coasian view of transnationals as firms that cross national boundaries, we therefore suggest the following.

A firm is the means of coordinating production from one centre of strategic decision-making.

A transnational is the means of coordinating production from one centre of strategic decision-making when this coordination takes a firm across national boundaries.

To compare and contrast our definition with the Coasian alternative, consider a simple illustration. Suppose an economy is characterised by one consumption good being produced without any market exchange and under the coordination of an operation with centralised strategic decision-making. Assume also that in production managers administrate and workers are employed to perform designated tasks. In a Coasian world this operation would be a firm: it is the means of coordinating production, there is no market exchange, and therefore it is 'the means of coordinating production without using market exchange'. We too would see the operation as a firm, but because of the centralised strategic decision-making. Moreover the critical difference between the approaches is shown by relaxing one of the simplifying assumptions. Suppose now that there are market exchanges in production. For instance, if the consumption good is clothing, one stage of production may require the putting together of a sales catalogue containing a sample of the cloth used. One possibility is to assemble workers in a factory where they literally sit down and glue squares of cloth onto a piece of card. This would be a non-market activity. Another possibility is to subcontract the work to housewives looking for additional money.[10] This would involve a market exchange. For example a housewife may be contracted to carry out the task in consideration of one penny for each batch of 20 completed cards. Such an exchange would fall *outside* the ambit of a Coasian firm but *inside* the ambit of a firm as we see it. Our preference for this view is because production is still being coordinated from one centre of strategic decision-making whether or not there is a market exchange. In ignoring this, the Coasian approach denies the especially important role of strategic decision-making in coordinating production.[11] This Coasian concern with superficial attributes misrepresents the activities of firms and only leads to misunderstanding and error.

Subsequent chapters will explore the significance of our analysis in greater detail, for example when we examine the rise of transnationals and the international division of labour in Chapter 4. But for now, perhaps a specific example from the real world will also clarify our position.[12] Mitter (1986) describes the case of Benetton, a clothing producer with over 2500 shops worldwide and with an expected turnover for 1983 of over £200 million. Benetton is reported as employing something less than 2000 people in 'its' eight factories in northern Italy and in addition of giving work to a further 6000 (also in northern Italy) employed by the 200 small subcontractors making semi-finished clothes which are supplied to the eight main plants. Mitter refers to the skilled parts of the production process – such as designing, cutting and final ironing – being 'handled by Benetton' whilst the basic weaving and making up is done 'outside the company's plant'. The reason: Benetton can thereby cut costs, e.g. by benefiting from the lower costs of the small subcontractors. In contrast our view is that it is *a priori* artificial to separate Benetton's eight main plants from the 200 subcontractors. Rather, the transnational 'Benetton' should include market exchanges where they are coordinated from one centre of strategic decision-making – and Mitter at least leaves a strong suggestion that what she calls Benetton is indeed in control of its sub-contractors, i.e. does include the centre of strategic decision-making that encompasses the subcontractors' activities. Moreover the importance of this is shown by the consequent difference in numbers of production workers employed by Benetton throughout northern Italy – 8000 rather than 2000, an increase of 300 per cent on Mitter's observation.

Following on from this the potential quantitative importance of our definition in general terms can be explored by pursuing the subcontracting phenomenon still further.[13] Thus the extent of subcontracting across national borders is not something that is generally evidenced by detailed statistics – as Germidis (1980) observes in a study covering many countries throughout the world – but an exception is the USA, where some rough indication is available. Table 2.1 shows the value of US imports under tariff items 807.00 and 806.30, items which permit importers of certain (although not all)[14] manufactured articles to pay duty only on the value added abroad and not on the value of the articles' US parts or materials. (See Sharpston (1976) and Helleiner (1981) for a discussion.) Unfortunately for us, even these data are severely tainted by the possibility that a vertically integrated Coasian transnational could have imports falling within the tariff provisions; i.e. there need be no market exchange concerning articles subject to duty under items 807.000 and 806.30. Nevertheless the items are much wider than this and their magnitude at least suggests that the subcontracting issue warrants close attention. Thus from Table 2.1: the annual growth rate of such imports has been consistently very high, rarely below and usually well above 20 per cent; and by 1979, for instance, over

Table 2.1: *US imports under tariff items 807.00 and 806.30, 1966–79 ($m)[15]*

Year	Value	Rise on previous year (%)	Value as a percentage of the value of all dutiable imports
1966	953		6.0
1967	1035	8.6	6.3
1968	1554	50.1	7.5
1969	1839	18.3	8.1
1970	2208	20.1	8.5
1971	2766	25.3	9.1
1972	3409	23.2	9.4
1973	4247	24.6	10.4
1974	5372	26.5	11.2
1975	5161	− 3.9	7.9
1976	5722	10.9	6.8
1977	7188	25.9	6.9
1978	9735	35.4	8.0
1979	11938	22.6	11.6

Source: The value data are from Helleiner (1981) (and originally the US International Trade Commission) and the US Statistical Abstract.

11 per cent of total dutiable imports to the US came under 807.00 and 806.30.

This discussion of subcontracting also immediately points to an important practical difficulty with our definition: in seeking data on transnationals it will at least be extremely hard to identify the ambit of centres of strategic decision-making. For example, obtaining data from the accounts of the firm legally identified as Benetton is insufficient as this will ignore subcontractors. This practical difficulty is also revealed by the complex and on-going debate regarding who makes strategic decisions. For example, suppose an individual controls production facilities in the US and also has 5 per cent of shares in sóme UK production facilities. Does the person control the UK facilities? – if so, there is a transnational producing in the US and UK because we have the coordination of production from one centre of control, in other words, from one centre of strategic decision-making. The answer to the question varies according to whose view is believed. For instance Berle and Means (1932) argue that a 20 per cent shareholding is needed for control, Scott and Hughes (1976) that 5 per cent suffices, Cubbin and Leech (1983) that the critical percentage varies and as little as 1 per cent may be enough, and Pitelis and Sugden (1986) that ex post analysis of shareholding is not revealing anyway.[16]

But there are two comments we shall make here. First, Coasian analysis also suffers from a practical problem. For instance suppose the production of chalk is coordinated within an institution named Problem Investments Limited solely by a set of non-market exchanges, whilst the production of cheese is coordinated within an institution named Worrying Factors Incorporated, again solely by a set of non-market exchanges. When are Problem Investments Limited and Worrying Factors Incorporated two firms, and when might they constitute one diversified firm? This is quite simply unclear and not uncontroversial. For instance, would there necessarily be only one firm if either Problem Investments or Worrying Factors owned part – say 40 per cent – of the other? Or 10 per cent, or even 1 per cent? Is there a critical percentage ? Or would there be one firm if both Problem Investments and Worrying Factors were owned by the same group of 20 individuals? Or 30? And suppose we simply do not know and cannot find out who owns what – after all, secret ownership is hardly a rarity.

Secondly, the problem should not be overemphasised; in a sense it is no problem at all. From a theoretical perspective the aim in defining a transnational is to isolate a concept which can be used to explore important issues from a theoretical standpoint. Without empirical exploration such work would have little value. However, when it comes to empirical application we must simply take account of limited data and appropriately qualify our conclusions. This is far better than the making of apparently sound conclusions based upon inadequate concepts; such an approach would only be deceptive.

WHY DO TRANSNATIONAL CORPORATIONS ARISE?

The key to understanding what is really going on when

transnationals come into existence is to appreciate the environment in which firms operate.

The typical view amongst economists is that firms operate in a more or less perfectly competitive environment. This is true of Coasian analysis, which focuses on the replacement of imperfect markets with non-market transactions yielding the perfectly competitive outcome of Pareto-efficiency. The view is sometimes relaxed after a while but usually as an appendix, given little thrust and, significantly, as an aberration from the competitive norm. The problem with it is that it flies in the face of all that firms are attempting to accomplish, assuming they are profit-maximisers. Thus firms in perfectly competitive markets merely achieve normal profits, which they will undoubtedly find unsatisfactory. Clearly, then, they will attempt to avoid such competition; i.e. they will try to dominate product markets and, in the extreme, obtain pure monopoly profits. Moreover if they succeed the competition view is misplaced.

That firms can dominate product markets is revealed by the possibility of their colluding. This concept is discussed in relation to pricing by Baran and Sweezy (1966):

The typical giant corporation . . . is one of several corporations producing commodities which are more or less adequate substitutes for each other. When one of them varies its price, the effect will be felt by the others. If firm A lowers its price, some new demand will be tapped, but the main effect will be to attract customers away from firms B, C and D. The latter, not willing to give up their business to A, will retaliate by lowering their prices, perhaps even undercutting A. While A's original move was made in the expectation of increasing its profit, the net result may be to leave all the firms in a worse position . . .

Unstable market situations of this sort . . . are anathema to the big corporations . . . To avoid such situations therefore becomes the first concern of corporate policy . . . (p. 57)

The crucial basic principle is that no firm will act in a way which leaves itself worse off, bearing in mind the retaliation of rivals. Thus collusion amongst firms is simply the avoidance of behaviour which leaves each and every firm worse off and it derives from recognition of the 'retaliatory power' of rivals. Whilst, if circumstances allowed, a firm would not hesitate to become a pure monopolist by driving rivals from the industry, more generally it cannot do this and will therefore accommodate their presence. Likewise a firm will appreciate that rivals tolerate its presence in the market because of its retaliatory power.

In short, then, our alternative characterisation of a firm's environment is as follows: collusive behaviour existing alongside and deriving from a ready willingness by each firm to drive rivals from the market – i.e. the coexistence of rivalry and collusion, as Cowling (1982) puts it. Moreover a lynchpin in such a world is firms' retaliatory power and thus their realisation that whilst they must *defend* against rivals (i.e. prevent others gaining profits at their expense) firms can also try to *attack* (i.e. improve their profits to the detriment of rivals).[17] This is crucial to our analysis because it suggests two motivations for firms' actions and thus two sets of reasons explaining the existence of transnationals: defending against and attacking rivals.

Defence can be illustrated by a scenario based upon (although slightly different to)[18] the view developed in Knickerbocker (1973), also discussed in Vernon (1977) with reference to the 'extraordinary proliferation' of foreign-owned producers of cars, consumer electronics and tyres in 'comparatively small and isolated' Latin American and Asian markets. Suppose there are two companies, which we shall call Bold Ventures Limited and Tricky Situations Incorporated. Both initially supply the UK market from factories abroad; but assume that Bold Ventures then becomes a transnational by subcontracting production to UK workers (compare the Coasian view). Tricky Situations Incorporated could see its rival's move as posing important risks which may induce it to match the move and also subcontract to the UK. The reason is that these risks refer to any factor influencing Bold Ventures' ability to drive Tricky Situations from the market, or at least to force a new situation in which Tricky Situations obtains reduced profits. For instance, producing in the UK may yield lower costs – perhaps because of cheaper factors of production – and these may enable Bold Ventures to undercut its rival in a successful price war from which it emerges a pure monopolist. Other scenarios could be given, and indeed in analysing the risk concept we could bring into play much of the existing literature on transnationals.[19] But the general point should already be clear: firms will become transnationals to consolidate their retaliatory power and thereby prevent loss to rivals.

Closely associated with this is attacks leading to transnationals. Thus whilst we have not discussed why Bold Ventures made the initial move to produce in the UK, following Yamin (1980) – who presents a general framework based upon rivalry but differing fundamentally to ours because he ignores collusion and accepts the 'monopolistic advantage' concept associated with Hymer (1960) and Kindleberger (1969)[20] – it could be that the firm was attempting to obtain advantages enabling it to gain at the expense of its rival, that is, the initial move may have been an attack.[21] This simply means that the factors underlying the fears that lead to defence also underlie firms becoming transnationals to gain from rivals. For example, in setting up UK production, Bold Ventures may have been seeking lower costs and hence the ability to push Tricky Situations from the market.[22]

Furthermore an alternative and revealing perspective on these points is given by the converse of the question we have been asking. Rather than ask why transnationals arise, we could ask why they do not. The obvious and immediate answer is because there is no need for defensive action or there are no attacking opportunities. But more can be said. A firm will not become a transnational if it believes the response of a rival will leave it worse off. For instance neither Bold Ventures nor Tricky Situations would become a transnational if they believed each other's retaliation would result in their obtaining lower profits – they will avoid such situations, they will collude. Indeed it could be that the reason there are no defensive or attacking moves is because collusion amongst firms is so strong that they agree to divide the world amongst themselves – to parcel it out, as Knickerbocker (1973) says. This avoids a situation where the firms would all be worse off as a result of defensive and attacking moves. Perhaps Bold Ventures, with the agreement of its rival, will concentrate all of its activity in the UK whilst in return Tricky Situations concentrates all of its activity in the United States. Indeed this would be very similar to an agreement reached at the turn of

the century in the cigarette and tobacco industry. (See Monopolies Commission, 1961.) The US-owned American Tobacco
Company and the UK-owned Imperial Tobacco Company
agreed not to trade in each other's home markets and only to
export elsewhere via the newly formed British American
Tobacco Company, which they owned jointly. This reveals
very clearly how collusion amongst rivals is at the heart of our
framework.[23]

The significance of this framework is that it is built upon
oligopolistic pursuit of profits. Transnationals arise because
they are a means of consolidating or increasing profits in an
oligopoly world. This need not yield Pareto-efficient outcomes. Take the case of Tricky Situations Incorporated
initially supplying the UK from its US factory, where it
employs individual I, a typical worker. The firm must decide
whether or not to match its rival in acquiring UK production
facilities. Suppose it does and consequently that Tricky Situations cuts back its US facilities, no longer employing I. The
vital point is that this worker's welfare may consequently
decline; then the transnational is *not* a Pareto-efficient outcome. The reason is that in the world we are depicting there is
a tendency towards unemployment and evidence suggests
workers prefer to be employed. The tendency towards unemployment is an issue we focus on in Chapter 5, where it is
argued that a world dominated by transnationals will be
plagued by stagnation. That workers dislike unemployment is
suggested by Payne *et al.*'s (1983) UK survey of roughly 400
unemployed males. More than 90 per cent agreed with the
statements 'Having a job is very important to me' and 'I hate
being on the dole'. This is confirmed by Field (1979), who
reports that in 1977 some 640,000 people in the UK lived in
households receiving income below supplementary benefit
level despite the household receiving a wage from full-time
work. The crucial fact is that a firm matching its rival is
concerned with profit and not the fate of its dismissed workers
– or anybody else for that matter.[24] Matching will increase
profits – otherwise a firm will not match; matching may de-
crease a worker's utility – this simply will not enter the firm's
calculation.

Thus we have not been developing a shallow alternative to

Coasian internalisation analysis; the two views have starkly different implications for welfare.

What allows this situation to arise is the distribution of decision-making within a firm – in particular the absence of democracy[25] and the dominance of an elite group. The fundamental behaviour of a firm is determined by the making of strategic-decisions, which include decisions over a firm's relationship with rivals and its geographical orientation – for example whether or not it is to become a transnational. Such decisions are taken by a firm's controllers despite resistance from others (see again Zeitlin (1974)). Moreover the whole basis of much, indeed most, economics is decisions made in the pursuit of selfish interest with no regard for others.[26] In line with this, then, once we have assumed a firm's fundamental behaviour is characterised by profit-maximisation – in other words, that controllers seek profits – our argument should come as no surprise: firms will become transnationals to pursue profits in a rivalry and collusion environment, an environment which follows from the profit maximising assumption. This is simply a consequence of controllers pursuing their selfish interests. The profit maximising assumption is clearly a critical link in our argument. However, it is quite general in the sense that it is perfectly consistent with various views on who controls firms, for example that control is in the hands of managers, some or even all shareholders.[27] Furthermore a common element in these views of control is that it is not in the hands of workers. Accordingly it should also be unsurprising when we argue that a firm becoming a transnational is unconcerned with worker welfare, for instance with the possibility of unemployment.

The fact is that workers do not take strategic decisions. If they did they could make the decisions suit their interests and for example consider the possibility of unemployment. As it is there is little they can do – controllers determine a firm's fundamental behaviour despite resistance from others, be these workers or anybody else. In such a situation workers have no real veto over outcomes they find undesirable. At most, they can attempt to dissuade transnational production by agreeing to changed working conditions – for example, accepting such low wages, and thereby cutting employers' costs, that production in one country is found by controllers to be the most profitable choice. But it may simply be that no wage sufficient to live on is low enough to have an influence, or that when negotiating, workers do not believe firms will produce elsewhere unless lower wages are accepted. Yet if they are wrong, transnationals will arise.

In short, the economy is not made up of voluntary exchanges yielding Pareto-efficient outcomes (compare the Coasian view). Rather, an awful lot rests in the hands of the dominant controllers, similarly to it being in their hands to decide whether to use market or non-market exchanges when coordinating production.

All of this leaves specific reasons for the existence of transnationals untouched. We have been developing a framework – talking in general terms of defence, attack, etc. – but within this we have not yet pursued any particular reason in any detail. We will in fact be taking this up in Chapter 4 in an examination of bargaining, labour costs and hence the existence of transnationals. The latter is an important task but it should be realised that it is at least as important to be perfectly clear regarding the perspective being adopted. Hence our concern here with establishing a framework. The perspective colours all that follows from it and is therefore fundamentally significant. Indeed this is a lesson that we have taken on board from Coasian analysis. However another way in which we have maintained the concerns of internalisation is to confine ourselves to developing microeconomic foundations for the existence of transnationals; this is all very well but does lack a macro viewpoint. Again we shall take this up later. Chapter 5 looks at macroeconomic issues, including the point that stagnationist tendencies in a particular country will cause firms to seek investment elsewhere, a point also discussed in Pitelis (1986). But for now, we shall content ourselves with having tackled the micro issues, confronted the prevailing orthodoxy and suggested an alternative.

NOTES

1. 'Outside the firm, price movements direct production, which is co-ordinated through a series of exchange transactions on the market. Within a firm, these market transactions are eliminated and in place of the complicated market structure with exchange transactions is substituted the entrepreneur co-ordinator, who directs production' (Coase (1937), p. 333).
2. Tomlinson (1984) in fact makes the general comment that neoclassical theories of the firm – in which tradition he includes the likes of Williamson (1975), a book drawing heavily on Coase (1937) – have the primary purpose of analysing markets rather than production.
3. The Coasian analysis also focuses on firms solely as a means of coordinating production. As a *first approximation* this seems reasonable and accordingly we shall follow the same line. However in reality it could be that firms are a means of consuming goods and services. For example it could be that a managing director's tax deductible expense account enables him to consume lavish dinners considerably more cheaply than if he simply ate as an individual. Compare also Hirshleifer (1976), for instance, asserting that consumption is 'engaged in *only* by natural individuals' (p. 15). This runs into the issue of managerialism (see for instance Williamson, 1964).
4. See more generally the review of theories of the firm in Tomlinson (1984).
5. See also Caves (1982).
6. Dunning (1977; 1979; 1980; 1981) has proposed an 'eclectic theory' which requires (among other things) that internalisation of activities is preferable to market coordination, *and* that a firm has a 'monopolistic advantage' over rivals. This contrasts with our interpretation of the literature: internalisation, on its own, explains the existence of firms, including transnationals. Casson (1980) supports our view. The monopolistic advantage concept comes from the interpretation of Hymer (1960) by Kindleberger (1969), see note 16.
7. Williamson (1975) notes (p. 248): 'The shift of transactions from autonomous market contracting to hierarchy is principally explained by the transactional economies that attend such assignments'. In examining different ways of organising the firm Williamson also discusses strategic decision-making, a concept central to the analysis we will be developing – see also Williamson (1970) and Chandler (1962), very influential in Williamson's work.
8. See also the literature in the organisational behaviour tradition, e.g. Drucker (1961), Channon (1979) and Andrews (1980).
9. See for example the review in Scott (1985).
10. Berthomieu and Hanaut (1980) note: 'Subcontracting can be defined briefly as "an operation whereby one undertaking (the principal) entrusts another (the subcontractor) with the task of performing on its behalf and according to a pre-established schedule of conditions a part

of the production activities for which it retains final economic responsibility" (report by J. J. Stephanelly to France's Conseil Economique et
Social, 21 March 1973' (p. 374).

11. (i) It is also instructive to relax two more of the assumptions underlying
our simple illustration. First, suppose there is more than one centre of
strategic decision-making. Then there are as many firms as there are
centres. Moreover the centres will be linked by market exchanges; after
all, each centre is involved in the production of the consumption good
and they therefore must be involved in interdependent activities (see
Buckley and Casson, 1976). Secondly, suppose there is more than one
consumption good being produced. This simply allows one centre of
strategic decision-making (i.e. one firm) to be associated with the
production of more than one consumption good. (Our only remaining
assumptions to consider concern managers administrating and workers
being employed to perform designated tasks. Their realism implies there
should be no difficulties with these.) (ii) The control concept has not
always been ignored in the transnationals literature. For instance Hood
and Young (1979): 'A multinational enterprise is a corporation which
owns (in whole or in part), controls and manages income-generating
assets in more than one country' (p. 3). Similarly for Ghertman and
Allen (1984): 'a multinational company . . . is "any company originating
in one country and housing continuous activities under its control in at
least two other countries, that is, foreign countries, which produce more
than ten per cent of total group turnover"' (p. 2). Interesting though
these are, their drawback is that they are not definitions that have been
well-founded in the theory of the firm, unlike our suggestion. (See also
Machlup (1967) and Sawyer (1981).)

12. See also the case of giant Japanese firms, as discussed in Imai and Itami
(1984), for example.

13. See also Cowling (1986).

14. 'Evidently, not all products which involve international subcontracting
will necessarily qualify under these customs items . . . As one example,
American cloth cut in the United States but sewn abroad qualifies under
807.00, but American cloth cut and sewn abroad would not qualify'
(Sharpston (1980) p. 95–6). There is also a further problem with the
data, according to Helleiner (1981), because of the possibility that 'some
of the subcontractors formerly did not take advantage of these tariff
concessions and have now begun to do so' (p. 37); the explanation for
this possible change is unclear.

15. The data refer to the total and not merely the dutiable value.

16. It is also worth noting the comment in Hood and Young (1979) that
transnational definitions incorporating the concept of control (see again
note 7(ii)) have used 25 per cent as the critical shareholding percentage.
This is extreme by all of the aforementioned standards.

17. See also such corporate strategy literature as Porter (1985).

18. Knickerbocker (1973) sees firms pursuing a risk-minimising strategy.
He has been criticised by Buckley and Casson (1976) on the fundamental grounds that the objectives of firms are never clearly stated. This is

correct. It is not certain why he posits risk-minimisation. Moreover, whilst firms will not undertake unnecessary risks, the minimisation hypothesis goes too far. It implies that if a risk can be avoided it will not be taken no matter what the potential rewards. In reality, whilst firms may be risk-averse, as Rugman (1975; 1977) suggests, it seems likely they will take some risks. Nevertheless, Knickerbocker's analysis can be translated to suit a world in which firms are not risk-minimisers. This we have done.

19. In analysing the risks in not matching rivals, determinants of production cost and demand are vital. Of relevance, therefore, is much of the existing literature on transnationals, albeit a literature not in line with the general framework being presented here. Thus significant costs, according to the existing literature, include: raw materials, see Hilferding (1910); transport, see Vernon (1974); taxes, see Caves (1971). As regards demand, the argument runs that if a firm produces a good where it is marketed it can be better adapted to local tastes (see Vernon, 1966, Caves, 1971 and Macewan, 1972). Note also Vernon's (1972) view that the analysis merely requires Bold Ventures and Tricky Situations to be rivals, not that they both supply the UK initially. For instance, they may both serve the USA and Bold Ventures' move into UK production may cause Tricky Situations to fear it can supply the US more cheaply. (See also Graham, 1978.) Furthermore firms will also keep an eye on potential rivals, who must also be defended against; thus they will seek entry barriers.

20. We are not restricted by the view that a 'monopolistic advantage' is necessary for a firm to produce in various countries. To illustrate the argument, consider firm A, with its administrative headquarters and only production facilities in the UK. Suppose A contemplates acquiring production facilities in the USA, over 3000 miles away. Kindelberger (1969) notes: 'There are costs of operating at a distance, costs not only of travel, communication, and time lost in communicating information and decisions, but also costs of misunderstanding that leads to errors' (p. 12). These costs would not be faced, for example, by firm B, with its administrative headquarters and only production facilities in the US. Thus, with perfect international markets in technology, factor inputs, and products, B would always prevent A from acquiring US production facilities. If firm A does acquire such facilities, there must be a market imperfection; put another way, A must have a 'monopolistic advantage' over existing or potential US firms. Assuming firms do face costs of operating at a distance, Kindelberger's analysis is correct, by definition of perfect markets. However, if there are no costs of operating at a distance the analysis is undermined. Moreover Buckley (1981) has argued, quite reasonably, that established transnationals have developed techniques to counter distance costs, which they do not therefore incur. Accordingly, a Hymer/Kindleberger approach cannot explain the activity of established transnationals. In contrast, whereas Kindelberger begins with costs of operating at a distance and concludes that markets must be imperfect, our analysis begins with imperfect

markets and concludes with implications for why there are transnationals. Furthermore, whilst admittedly it talks of firms 'becoming transnationals' etc., in this sense focusing on the decision of a firm initially producing in one country to produce in more than one, clearly our analysis is in fact more general and applies even when a firm initially produces in various countries. Thus it explains the activities of established transnationals. And we cannot be criticised on the grounds that established transnationals do not incur costs of operating at a distance, such costs not being a critical issue. Although the view contained in Buckley (1981) is at least a reasonable hypothesis, it remains true that established transnationals operate in a world of imperfect markets, and it is this that leads to the acquisition of production facilities in various countries.

21. If the initial move is not aimed at gaining profits at its rival's expense, it must be defensive. A firm may move first to preempt an expected attack by a rival. (See Yamin (1980) once more.)

22. A theoretical possibility for a third set of reasons explaining the existence of transnationals considers a firm attempting to increase profits but with no regard for doing so at the expense of rivals and without worrying about defence. In practice, however, this will be a non-starter, simply because of the critical importance of defence and attack in the world we are depicting. Defence and attack will always be uppermost in a firm's mind; that is the nature of the world in which it operates.

23. This also suggests the possibility of firms dividing the world into areas spanning countries – e.g. Bold Ventures takes Europe, Tricky Situations takes North America. Then, if Bold Ventures produced in several European countries our framework could offer little real explanation, although such a case of pure monopoly covering various countries could easily be accommodated within the 'divide-and-rule' analysis of Chapter 4. But in practice this will not be a common or general case and it can therefore be reasonably confined to the realms of theory. In reality the norm will be for more than one firm to operate in a given area, in which case our framework will apply. This reflects the more general proposition that oligopoly is ubiquitous; in the context of the world economy pure monopoly is to all intents and purposes absent, especially when the possibility of potential rivals is taken into account.

24. Examples could also be given of firms becoming transnational and others losing utility regardless of unemployment. Consider, for instance, consumers. A hornets' nest of controversy surrounds, for example, the consequences for consumer utility of product differentiation. Space constraints alone prevent these issues from being explored here. However, one example illustrates the view that transnationals may arise to the detriment of consumer utility. Thus, consider the case of a firm acquiring production facilities in various countries to prevent potential rivals from entering its industry – e.g. the firm secures vital raw material supplies. The entry barriers (at least could) imply a higher product price than would otherwise be the case. Assuming their money

incomes are unchanged, consumers of the firm's products are therefore worse off.

25. Democracy is an issue pursued in Chapter 6 in some detail.

26. See also Tomlinson (1984) for a critical discussion of groups pursuing their interests in various theories of the firm.

27. There is a detailed discussion in Cowling (1982) of the consistency between profit maximisation and managerialism, reflected in intra-corporate consumption out of non-reported profits. More generally on control and firm's objectives, see Pitelis and Sugden (1986).

3 The Influence of Transnationals in the Monopolisation of Product Markets

One of the things we have been discussing is how, given firms' desire to monopolise product markets, transnationals may arise. In doing so retaliatory power was identified as a crucial concept and the economist's traditional focus on efficient outcomes was overturned. The aim now is to build upon this by considering how, given the presence of transnationals, they may influence the monopolisation of product markets.

Our starting-point is to consider evidence illustrating the position of transnationals in the UK economy. In particular we look at their total market shares. The purpose of this is to give an example of the extent of transnationals' importance in one of the world's major economies; after all, if transnationals are to have any meaningful influence on monopolisation they must be shown to have a significant presence. It is therefore a worthwhile, even obvious, thing to do. Yet it encounters difficulties which are in themselves revealing of our unorthodox approach. Down the years a great deal of interesting information has been reported about the importance of transnationals. But it is curious that in countries like the UK there has also been a tendency to ignore certain activities. The focus has been on UK-registered transnationals outside the UK and non-UK-registered transnationals inside the UK, not transnationals in the UK. This probably reflects the issues that have worried researchers; namely, the problems, costs and benefits of so-called 'home' and 'host' countries. Yet for us this is deficient.[1] Our worry is the activities of *all* transnationals within a given product market – only then can we examine its monopolisation. Accordingly, in considering the UK example, we shall break from the traditional tendency but will be limited by the quality and quantity of available information.

Whilst evidence of transnationals' market share is interesting, however, it cannot tell the full story of their influence. To simply say they have a large market share suggests they are important but nevertheless leaves open whether or not this is actually true. Thus we shall go on to explore how a significant presence actually does affect monopolisation.

The measure of monopoly analysed will be the price–marginal cost margin, also known as the degree of monopoly because a rise in the margin is associated with increasing monopolisation (see Scherer (1980) for instance). It is certainly not our only available option but we shall be in good company as it has received a lot of attention from many authors, largely because non-zero margins imply allocative inefficiency and also have implications for income distribution. It is the inefficiency issue that has captured most attention in the existing literature but for us income distribution is particularly interesting, because of its welfare impact.

Whereas in the previous chapter we focused on the unemployment aspect of distribution here the concern is the share going to wages. This can be illustrated by considering an industry's price–marginal cost margin, which we will denote by μ. μ can be seen as a weighted average of each firm's margin with the weights being given by the firm's share in total market sales. Then, following the pioneering work of Kalecki (1971), if firms are assumed to face constant marginal costs μ is actually the ratio of industry profits (Π) and fixed costs (F) to total revenue (V). That is: $\mu = (\Pi + F)/V$. This is shown in detail by Cowling (1982), where for instance the constant marginal costs assumption is justified as realistic. Moreover this is easily translated into an expression for income shares – again the details can be pursued in Cowling (1982). Assume costs comprise solely raw material and wage bills. Denote value added as Y, where this comprises Π plus F plus total wages, W. Then substituting into the expression for μ and rearranging we obtain:[2]

$$\frac{W}{Y} = 1 - \mu\frac{V}{Y} \quad \text{and} \quad \frac{\Pi + F}{Y} = \mu\frac{V}{Y}$$

W/Y is the share of wages in value added. Thus for wage share to change there must be an alteration in μ and/or V/Y, which Cowling (1982) explains is the same as requiring an alteration in μ and/or the ratio of wages bill to materials expenditure.[3] Hence the price–cost margin is clearly crucial. For instance if the wages : materials ratio is constant, a rise in μ will imply a fall in wages share or, put another way, a rise in wage share must be accompanied by a fall in μ. A similar analysis also applies to $(\Pi + F)/Y$. This is the share of 'gross capitalist income plus salaries' since $\Pi + F$ is made up of profit plus interest, rent, depreciation and salaries (which together comprise F).

Yet despite such attention being given to the price–cost margin, the effects of transnationals have been largely ignored in the existing literature[4] and there is consequently a gap that needs filling. Towards this end we shall therefore develop and evaluate a traditional structure conduct performance model that accommodates transnationals' existence. In so doing we shall be considering a currently influential way of analysing price–cost margins. But this will not be the finish of our analysis. Indeed the section could be omitted with little loss of continuity in our overall argument because it rejects the model as inadequate. Our criticisms will lead us beyond it to explore the real causal factors in determining price-cost margins, most notably the retaliatory power of firms, and to consider particular issues raised by transnationals in this respect. We shall then conclude with the implication that can be drawn for monopolisation from our evidence on transnationals' market share in the UK.

THE MARKET SHARE OF TRANSNATIONALS IN THE UK ECONOMY

The most readily available, useable information on transnationals' market share is contained in Census of Production Summary Tables. It reports the sales and employment of 'foreign enterprises' in UK manufacturing. The data for 1975–81 is expressed as shares of total UK manufacturing in Table 3.1.[5] Similarly Tables 3.2 and 3.3 report shares by sectors for the period 1975–79 (later years being omitted because of a change in Standard Industrial Classification). The clear picture is of non-UK-registered transnationals having a significant and growing presence. By 1975 they were responsible for 18.8 per cent of sales in manufacturing. This rose in 1977 and 1979 but dropped back in 1981, although at 19.41 per cent there was still a growth of over 3 per cent on the 1975 figure. As for total employment, their share grew continuously and by 1981 had reached 14.85 per cent, an increase on 1975 of nearly 20 per cent. Moreover whilst they increased their employment share in every sector, only in food, drink and tobacco was there a drop in their sales share.

These magnitudes are all the more significant given two major problems with the data. First, the Census of Production defines 'foreign enterprises' as effectively UK producers with at least 51 per cent of their shares owned by companies incorporated overseas.[6] This is a very narrow definition of a transnational and therefore the employment and sales shares will be underestimates. For instance it omits activity based upon subcontracting arrangements and requires a far higher

Table 3.1: Share of foreign enterprises in the sales and employment of total UK manufacturing, 1975–81 (%)

	1975	1977	1979	1981	Percentage change 1975–81
Sales	18.80	21.21	21.70	19.41	3.24
Employment	12.40	13.92	14.07	14.85	19.76

Source: Derived from Census of Production Summary Tables.

Table 3.2:   Share of foreign enterprises in the sales of total UK manufacturing, by sector, 1975–79 (%)

	1975	1977	1979	Percentage change 1975–79
Food, drink, tobacco	14.08	13.18	12.79	−9.16
Coal and petroleum products	58.01	65.38	67.28	15.98
Chemicals and allied industries	25.35	30.39	30.12	18.82
Metal manufacture	9.01	10.56	13.32	47.84
Mechanical engineering	19.59	20.04	21.41	9.29
Instrument engineering	29.71	32.90	33.59	13.06
Electrical engineering	22.83	24.91	25.16	10.21
Shipbuilding, marine engineering, vehicles	27.16	32.02	33.85	24.63
Other metal goods	9.80	13.21	13.83	41.12
Textiles	6.66	7.56	7.41	11.26
Leather, leather goods, fur, clothing, footwear	3.05	3.97	4.28	40.33
Bricks, pottery, glass, cement, etc.	8.00	10.79	8.27	3.38
Timber, furniture, etc.	1.17	2.98	2.32	98.29
Paper, printing, publishing	10.58	16.46	11.80	11.53
Others	21.55	24.56	23.97	11.23

Source: Derived from Census of Production Summary Tables.

shareholding than would generally be accepted as sufficient for control of the firm – even Berle and Means (1932) only require that an identifiable interest group holds 20 per cent and they are way out of line with current thinking. Secondly, the data refer to sales from and employment in UK production, not sales in the UK and not employment associated with sales in the UK. It consequently includes exports and excludes imports. Ideally it would refer to all UK sales as this would genuinely illustrate transnationals' importance in a given market. As it is a particular problem is the failure to pick up changes in the source of transnationals' sales. For example if a foreign enterprise *increased* sales of cars in the UK between 1975 and 1981 but over the same period reduced the number produced in the UK, this would appear in the data as a *reduction* in the sales of foreign enterprises. This is especially important given the world we are portraying. As will be seen in Chapter 5, this sees transnationals leading to deindustrialisation in the UK: i.e. they use investment finance generated by UK manufacturing to increase their production and hence employment overseas whilst these are reduced domestically, this process leading into a vicious downward spiral. Hence this implies UK product markets will be sourced from production elsewhere. In other words, whilst transnationals will continue to supply the UK, the rise in their overseas at the expense of their domestic production means an ever greater reliance on imports. Thus our share data will once again be biased, failing to pick up the true market share of non-UK-registered transnationals. With deindustrialisation it would be no surprise to see the estimated shares of foreign enterprises falling as a result of a rise in their overseas sourcing. As it is, their shares have certainly not fallen.

There are similar difficulties with the altogether more problematic UK-registered transnationals. These data are not as readily available. We have estimated the sales and employ-

Table 3.3: Share of foreign enterprises in the employment of total UK manufacturing, by sector, 1975–79 (%)

	1975	1977	1979	Percentage change, 1975–79
Food, drink, tobacco	10.26	10.34	10.67	4.00
Coal and petroleum products	30.58	33.92	33.93	10.95
Chemicals and allied industries	23.44	28.33	27.20	16.04
Metal manufacture	4.50	5.22	6.53	45.11
Mechanical engineering	16.08	16.04	17.59	9.39
Instrument engineering	25.76	29.05	29.37	14.01
Electrical engineering	19.55	20.38	20.28	3.73
Shipbuilding, marine engineering, vehicles	18.71	20.35	21.11	12.83
Other metal goods	7.95	9.42	9.80	23.27
Textiles	4.43	5.05	5.07	14.45
Leather, leather goods, fur, clothing, footwear	2.02	3.18	3.03	50.00
Bricks, pottery, glass, cement, etc.	7.48	10.96	7.99	6.82
Timber, furniture etc.	1.07	2.46	2.02	88.79
Paper, printing, publishing	8.51	12.26	9.69	13.97
Others	16.94	18.46	17.86	5.43

Source: Derived from Census of Production Summary tables.

ment of leading firms using the abbreviated company accounts in Stopford (1982) and Stopford, Dunning and Haberich (1980), two directories of transnational corporations. The firms are all UK-registered transnationals for which the directories give data for each of the years 1975, 1977, 1979 and 1981; our sample comprises 28 in the case of sales and 45 in the case of employment. The firms are listed according to their principal industry in the Statistical Appendix.

This is clearly a limited sample. Apart from data problems excluding some firms with entries in the directories, for a firm to be included in Stopford (1982) – and all in the samples have to be – it must meet one or more of the following criteria: have '25 per cent or more of the voting equity of manufacturing or mining companies in at least three foreign countries'; have 'at least 5 per cent of its consolidated sales or assets attributable to foreign investment'; have 'at least $75 million sales originating from foreign manufacturing operations'.[7] Again, this is clearly very restrictive as a definition of a transnational and therefore the sales and employment estimates far from cover all of the firms we are interested in.

Even ignoring this, both estimates include all activities of companies in so far as these are reflected in the accounts – they therefore may include activities outside manufacturing. Moreover the employment data refer simply to UK production; as with foreign enterprises it consequently reflects a firm's exports but not its imports. And as for the sales figures, they pose even more queries. On the one hand they merely approximate the total net sales by transnationals' UK divisions, including exports from the UK. The approximation is because net sales should really exclude trade within the firm, but sometimes intra-firm trade taints the reported information.[8] On the other hand, even an accurate figure for total net sales by UK divisions is not ideal; for instance, whilst comparability with Census of Production data suggests the inclusion of all exports, intra-firm as well as net, the sourcing problem implies it would be ideal to have information on all of transnationals' imports.

Despite all of these complexities, the estimated sales and employment data for our admittedly limited sample are nevertheless worth looking at. They at least provide some indication of what is going on. Accordingly Tables 3.4 and 3.5 show the sales and employment shares, respectively, of leading UK transnationals in total manufacturing for 1975–81.[9] For such a small number of firms the percentages are remarkably high; by 1981, 28 leading transnationals were responsible for nearly 17 per cent of total sales whereas 45 leading transnationals were responsible for nearly 28 per cent of employment. In both cases this represents a rise on 1975, although for employment this is barely significant and for neither is it smooth.

Table 3.4: Share of 28 leading UK transnationals in the sales of total UK manufacturing, 1975–81 (%)

1975	1977	1979	1981	Percentage change 1975–81
16.08	15.34	15.13	16.72	3.98

Source: Derived from data in Stopford (1982), Stopford, Dunning and Haberich (1980), and Census of Production Summary Tables.

What the tables are suggesting is the same sort of thing as Tables 3.1–3.3; transnationals are important in the UK and to a growing extent. This is also shown very clearly in Tables 3.6 and 3.7, which bring together the data for foreign enterprises and leading UK transnationals. They reveal a combined sales share of 36.13 per cent in 1981, a rise of 3.58 per cent compared to 1975. The combined employment share is a very high 42.56 per cent, an increase of nearly 7 per cent.

Table 3.5: Share of 45 leading UK transnationals in the employment of total UK manufacturing, 1975–81 (%)

1975	1977	1979	1981	Percentage change 1975–81
27.47	26.39	27.12	27.71	0.87

Source: Derived from data in Stopford (1982), Stopford, Dunning and Haberich (1980), and Census of Production Summary Tables.

Table 3.6:   Share of foreign enterprises and 28 leading UK transnationals in the sales of total UK manufacturing, 1975–81 (%)

1975	1977	1979	1981	Percentage change 1975–81
34.88	36.55	36.83	36.13	3.58

Source: Derived from data in Stopford (1982), Stopford, Dunning and Haberich (1980), and Census of Production Summary Tables.

Table 3.7:   Share of foreign enterprises and 45 leading UK transnationals in the employment of total UK manufacturing, 1975–81 (%)

1975	1977	1979	1981	Percentage change 1975–81
39.87	40.31	41.19	42.56	6.75

Source: Derived from data in Stopford (1982), Stopford, Dunning and Haberich (1980), and Census of Production Summary Tables.

A STRUCTURE CONDUCT PERFORMANCE MODEL INCORPORATING TRANSNATIONALS

In an attempt to pin down how this large, growing market share translates into an influence on monopolisation, transnationals can be analysed within a formal model that moves from firms' first-order conditions for profit-maximisation to an expression for the degree of monopoly. See for instance the development of such models (albeit ignoring transnationals) in Cowling and Waterson (1976) and Clarke and Davies (1982).

To show this, assume the following:

   (i)   a closed economy;
  (ii)   a homogeneous product industry, in which
 (iii)   there are T firms which are transnationals and N which only produce in one country – i.e. N which are national corporations;
  (iv)   each firm has zero fixed costs and constant marginal costs.

Whilst these are undoubtedly limiting assumptions their only effect is to simplify analysis and they in no way alter our conclusions. Thus the typical transnational, firm t, has profits of

$$pX_t - c_t X_t \tag{1}$$

where p is the product price, X_t the firm's output and c_t its marginal costs. The profit maximising first order condition is then:

$$p - c_t + X_t \frac{dp}{dX_t} = 0 \tag{2}$$

Hence rearrangement and manipulation yields an expression that has t's price–cost margin on the left-hand side:

$$\frac{p - c_t}{p} = \frac{-X_t}{p} \frac{dp}{dX} \frac{dX}{dX_t} \frac{X}{X} = \frac{1}{\varepsilon} S_t \frac{dX}{dX_t} \tag{3}$$

Here X is total market sales. Hence on the right-hand side we have firm t's market share, S_t, the absolute value of the industry elasticity of demand, ε, and the change in total output that t expects to result from a marginal change in its own output, dX/dX_t.

Moreover the Mathematical Appendix illustrates how (3) can be transformed into the following:

$$\frac{p - c_t}{p} = \frac{1}{\varepsilon}[\beta + (a - \beta)S_T + (1 - a)S_t] \tag{4}$$

where: S_T is the total market share of all transnationals; a and β are what are commonly called conjectural elasticities. a and β actually capture a transnational's expectation of the response of rivals to a marginal change in its output. a is a transnational's conjecture regarding the elasticity of a rival transnational's output with respect to a change in its own output; we assume, again merely for simplicity and without upsetting our conclusions, that each and every transnational holds the same conjecture for each and every rival transnational. Similarly β is the conjecture over the output of a rival national corporation. Thus equation (4) clearly relates the price–cost margin measure of a firm's performance to both structure and conduct; structure is seen in S_T and S_t; conduct is contained in a and β. In the same way, if we assume a typical national corporation also holds conjectural elasticities of a and β over transnational and national rivals respectively, its degree of monopoly is given by:

$$\frac{p-c_n}{p}=\frac{1}{\varepsilon}[\beta+(a-\beta)S_T+(1-\beta)S_n] \tag{5}$$

where: S_n is the market share of firm n (the typical national corporation).[10] Consequently equations (4) and (5) can be brought together to form an expression for an industry's weighted average degree of monopoly. This is also shown in the Mathematical Appendix and is as follows.

$$\mu \equiv \sum_{i=1}^{N+T} \frac{p-c_i}{p}\frac{X_i}{X}=\frac{\beta}{\varepsilon}+\frac{(1-\beta)}{\varepsilon}H$$

$$+\frac{(a-\beta)\ (1-S_TH_T)S_T}{\varepsilon} \tag{6}$$

where: H is the industry level Herfindahl index of concentration; H_T is the Herfindahl index of concentration amongst transnationals (i.e. $\sum_{t=1}^{T} \hat{S}_t^2$ where $\hat{S}_t$ is firm t's share in the total sales of all transnationals). This is the particularly interesting result for our purposes as it allows us to focus on the role of transnationals at the level of a particular market.

The difference between equation (6) and normally reported expressions for μ is the last term on the right-hand side. Thus if transnationals are not focused upon as at least potentially important, no distinction is made between national and transnational corporations, hence a is seen as no different from β and the last term drops out, leaving:

$$\mu=\frac{\beta}{\varepsilon}+\frac{(1-\beta)}{\varepsilon}H \tag{7}$$

Here β merely represents a firm's conjecture over the elasticity of a rival's output with respect to a change in its own output, as explained in for instance Cowling (1981), Clarke and Davies (1982) and Dixit and Stern (1982). Yet recognising the distinction between firms introduces a term dependent upon both conduct – in the form of conjectures – and structure, including the market share of transnationals.

It is therefore tempting to conclude from equation (6) that S_T is a determinant of μ; we could then examine the effect of the large, growing S_T that was reported earlier. Unfortunately nothing is that simple and it would be wrong to pursue this line. The problem is that equation (6) merely describes an equilibrium and is virtually silent on causality.

One way of seeing this is to go back to equation (2), the building-block from which (6) was constructed, to explore the model in greater detail. Firm t's first-order condition for profit maximisation can be rewritten as a reaction function – i.e. t's profit-maximising output can be expressed as a function of rivals' outputs, with cost parameters, demand parameters and conjectures (which are included in the dp/dX_t term)[11] all being given.[12] This is illustrated in Figure 3.1 for the case of a duopoly facing a linear market demand curve. R_i, $i = 1, 2$ is firm i's reaction function. The idea is that if firm 2 produces an amount OA, firm 1 will respond by producing OB, the point on R_1 that corresponds to $X_2 = OA$. Moreover it will do so taking account of its rival's reactions; this is ensured by the presence of a conjecture term in the reaction function equation.

However in the general case this encounters an acute difficulty, as pointed out by Fellner (1949) and Stigler (1968). Given $X_1 = OB$, firm 2 will alter its output to OC and thereby cause its rival to cut output to OD. This clearly indicates to firm 1 that its original conjecture regarding rivals is wrong and should be changed. Yet this is not accommodated by the model. Furthermore such an undoubted contradiction cannot be allowed to persist simply because it is an inconsistency at the heart of the analysis. Accordingly the model needs to be interpreted in a way that overcomes the problem.

Whilst this is possible, the penalty is that it requires a very restrictive view preventing the model from saying what deter-

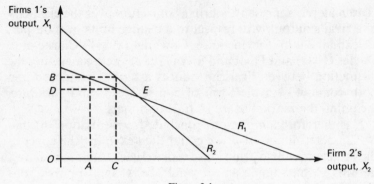

Figure 3.1
Reaction functions in a duopoly

mines performance. This is revealed by considering two responses to the contradiction.[13]

The first is to argue that the first-order profit-maximising conditions hold *only* when the industry is in a situation where no firm wishes to change its output, given the production of rivals – which is to say that they hold only when the industry is in Nash equilibrium. That the conditions do hold in such a situation follows immediately from the profit-maximising assumption; because no firm wishes to change its output, each firm must in fact be maximising its profits and therefore must be satisfying the maximising conditions. (That the conditions need not hold in other situations is suggested by the Fellner and Stigler point.) In terms of Figure 3.1 this implies that the first-order conditions apply *only* at *point E*; this is the only point at which no firm wishes to change its output given the production of its rival. This view leaves the model *per se* with comparatively little real value. To argue that first-order conditions – and hence the likes of equation (6) – hold only in Nash equilibrium is merely to describe such situations and to say virtually nothing about why they arise. Thus whereas it is clear that they are not determined by a set of simple reaction functions, it is not clear what they are determined by. The same is true when the second response is considered. Thus it could be argued that the oligopoly model is simply an 'as if' approach – i.e. that it is as if the duopolists behave according to reaction functions R_1 and R_2. But what does an 'as if' approach mean? To say something is 'as if' is not to say what it really is; for instance to say firms behave as if there are reaction functions is not to say how or why they do behave.

In short, then, the model has not put any determinant of the degree of monopoly in issue. It is analogous to observing a series of buckets containing different amounts of water and measuring the amount in each; the measuring describes a situation but *per se* says little about the determinants of the water level. Yet if we want to examine transnationals' influence in monopolisation the causal factors must be unearthed. A much deeper analysis is called for.

Having said this the formal model is not a complete waste of time and when put in its proper context does provide a starting-point. The Fellner and Stigler criticism follows from the model's mathematical properties; the suggestion that firms adhere to a particular equation leads to the drawing of reaction functions and hence the recognition of a contradiction. This is all very well but it should not be forgotten that a reason such formal models were initially so exciting was precisely because they attempted to formalise an even longer tradition of oligopoly modelling that goes back to the 1930s (see for instance the discussions in Scherer (1980) and Donsimoni, Geroski and Jacquemin (1984)). This tradition argues, for example, that performance is determined by conduct, and conduct is determined by structure. (Compare also the narrow view of Clarke and Davies (1982) on the likes of equation (2).)[14] Thus the concern of the formal model with structure, conduct and performance is well founded and seems worth maintaining. Indeed there is something obvious and therefore appealing about trying to explain performance by focusing on conduct; it is certainly plausible to expect a firm's behaviour to determine how it performs. Accordingly we shall pursue this line of thought.

THE DETERMINANTS OF PRICE–COST MARGINS

Stigler (1968) offers a basic principle that should guide an examination of the behaviour underlying a firm's actions. He suggests that a fundamental problem with the conjecture models we have been discussing is that behaviour is postulated rather than deduced from profit maximisation; i.e. conjectures are simply fed into first-order conditions as parameters. Yet what should happen, Stigler argues, is something very different:

profit-maximising must imply the form of behaviour – economic behaviour is a means to achieve this end, not a separate part of man to be supplied by a psychiatrist or a sociologist. (p. 36)

As with our analysis of why transnationals exist, this again suggests that the collusion concept be put on centre stage.

Because firms desire profits they will avoid perfect competition and seek monopoly positions – firms will look to increase their monopolisation of markets, in the extreme case obtaining a position of pure monopoly. They will *therefore* collude. That is, recognition of each other's retaliatory power means firms will tolerate each other's presence in the market to the extent of avoiding situations which leave each and every one of the firms in a worse position.[15] Otherwise they would simply be cutting their own throats by being worse off and suicidal tendencies are not a general feature of firms' behaviour. Rather their concern is normally to protect their own skins at all costs. We have already seen this in Chapter 2 when looking at Baran and Sweezy's (1966) discussion of giant firms' pricing behaviour. Similarly Scherer (1980) notes:

When the number of sellers is small, each firm recognises that aggressive action such as price cutting will induce counteractions from rivals which, in the end, leave all members of the industry worse off. All may therefore exercise mutual restraint and prevent prices from falling to the competitive level. (p. 514)

Moreover, although Baran and Sweezy refer to giant firms and Scherer to industries with few sellers, this is unnecessarily restrictive.[16] Collusion derives from recognition of interdependence and thus characterises all industries. The presence or absence of such conduct is not determined by, for instance, structure. It is simply a given feature. After all an industry by definition comprises firms producing goods which are substitutes for each other, and so interdependence is a fact.[17] There is no reason to think this is not recognised by firms[18] and every reason to think that it is; it is hard to believe firms could operate in an industry without appreciating their interdependence.

Collusion, then, is the key feature of firms' conduct. But because it characterises all industries its presence or absence *cannot* determine performance – quite simply it is always present. However, the consequences of collusion *can* vary across industries and this will be reflected in observed price-cost margins.

The polar case of ultimate success for colluders is joint profit-maximisation. This is because firms seek profits and collectively they can never obtain more than at the joint maximum. As Baran and Sweezy (1966) comment:

sellers of a given commodity or of close substitutes have an interest in seeing that the price or prices established are such as to maximise the profits of the group as a whole. (p. 68)

Thus profit-maximisation suggests the benchmark for analysing an industry's performance is most sensibly the case of monopoly, where price and price–cost margin – given by $\mu = 1/\varepsilon$ – are generally accepted to be at their highest. But this can only be a benchmark. Whilst some, perhaps many industries may achieve joint maximisation, departures from it elsewhere must be explained. The basis for this remains the collusion concept. If firms are not maximising joint profits it is because at least one firm (believes it)[19] is better off not doing so; if this is not true they are all worse off – because collectively profits must be less – and they would collude, thereby avoiding this outcome. Moreover for our purposes the most interesting possibility of a firm gaining by not maximising joint profits derives from a cut in price yielding increased profits.

This can be usefully illustrated and explored using a simple example.[20] Suppose firm *i* cuts its price at time zero. The change in its profits depends crucially upon when and how rivals respond. Generally response is not immediate because it takes time both to detect price cuts (as is clear from Stigler,

1964, for example) and to formulate the desired response. Thus initially the price cut will generally yield i increased profits as it will simply give i the new buyers that are attracted to the industry and new buyers attracted from rivals – which is again clear from Stigler (1964), and also from Baran and Sweezy (1966). But when rivals do respond they will cut their prices in an attempt to attract back buyers from firm i and thereby re-establish profits.[21] (See for instance the analysis of Osborne (1976) and the comment on this in Holohan (1978).) As a consequence firm i's profits will fall again. This is depicted in Figure 3.2, where (at most for simplification)[22] we assume:

(a) rivals respond to i's price cut at time $\hat{t}$, after which neither i nor its rivals can alter their prices again;
(b) firm i is only concerned with profits until time $\hat{T}$;
(c) firm i knows with certainty the change in its profits both before and after rivals respond;
(d) buyers require no time to acquire information about new prices.

In the figure, Π_1 is i's profits per period without any cut in price, Π_2 is profits when it has cut price but rivals have not responded, and Π_3 is profits once they have responded. Accordingly the change in firm i's profits is given by the following expression:

$$\Delta\Pi_i = \hat{t}(\Pi_2 - \Pi_1) + (\hat{T} - \hat{t})(\Pi_3 - \Pi_1) \qquad (8)$$

The possibility of a price cut yielding increased profits therefore depends upon whether or not $\hat{t}(\Pi_2 - \Pi_1) + (\hat{T} - \hat{t})(\Pi_3 - \Pi_1) > 0$. This can be used to explore the determinants of a price cut. Whereas in practice firm i either will or will not cut its price, it is reasonable to claim that the lower is $\Delta\Pi_i$ the less likely is a cut (and vice versa). Using equation (8) to calculate the partial derivatives of $\Delta\Pi_i$ consequently yields generalisations regarding the likelihood of a price cut. For example *ceteris paribus* falls in both $\hat{t}$ and Π_3 make cuts less likely.[23]

The especially interesting feature of Figure 3.2 and equation (8) is the significance of when and how rivals respond. This is

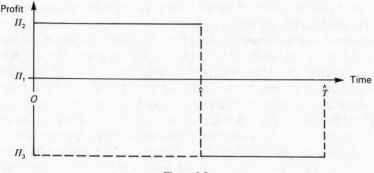

Figure 3.2
The time profile of firm i's profits

so important because it determines $\hat{t}$, hence the duration of initial profit gains and subsequent profit reductions, as well as Π_3, the magnitude of those reductions. Together $\hat{t}$ and Π_3 constitute rivals' retaliatory power; they are rivals' power to detect and respond, therefore to retaliate.[24] The conclusion is that the quicker the response and the greater the consequent loss – i.e. the greater the retaliatory power – the less likely is a cut in price. Furthermore this is simply another way of saying that retaliatory power means firms will collude. The reason greater retaliatory power makes a price cut less likely is because it implies a lower $\Delta\Pi_i$ and a cut will not be made where this leaves the firm worse off. Rather, the firm will avoid such a situation. Bearing in mind that this holds for all firms, they will tolerate each other's presence in the market to avoid situations where they are all worse off – they will collude.

Thus we have argued that profit-maximisation suggests the benchmark for analysing an industry's performance is monopoly, departures from this depending crucially upon the retaliatory power of firms. The implication is that an industry's degree of monopoly is essentially given by:

$$\mu = \frac{R}{\varepsilon}; \ 0 < R \leqslant 1$$

where R is an index of firms' retaliatory power. This sees the crucial determinants of μ as demand elasticity and retaliatory power.[25] The maximum value of R being unity picks up $\mu = 1/\varepsilon$ being the joint profit maximum. As for its lower bound, we can at least say that generally $R > 0$. This follows from the meaning of collusion. If firms are in a position where they *cannot* become worse off this *cannot* be the result of collusion – there are no worse situations to avoid. Yet firms do collude. Accordingly if we assume exit from an industry costs nothing and that each firm has constant marginal costs, it must be that $\mu > 0$, in other words $R > 0$. $\mu = 0$ (which requires $R = 0$) would imply zero price-cost margins for all firms. But this is the worst they could ever be in so far as a negative margin implies a failure to cover variable costs and therefore losses avoidable by exit.

Moreover, and most importantly for our purposes, equation (9) says that a rise in retaliatory power leads to a rise in μ. This is a simplification because it translates likelihoods into certainties. Its basis is the point that firms will not be maximising joint profits if at least one finds it profitable to cut its price, yet a rise in rivals' retaliatory power makes a profitable price cut less likely and hence the attainment of joint profit-maximisation more likely. Suppose, for instance, we observed the retaliatory power of firms in the shoe-making industry in 1975 and 1981. Assume the only difference between the years is that one firm, Lucky Boots Limited, has a higher level of retaliatory power in 1981 than in 1975. This will imply that all other firms will face a higher level of rivals' retaliatory power in 1981, and hence be less likely to cut price. Thus when Lucky Boots Limited has a higher level of retaliatory power R (and hence μ) will be higher. Similarly, if other things being equal more than one and even all firms have higher retaliatory power, R and therefore μ will be greater.

It is at this point that we can reintroduce structure into the argument and give it a leading role. Again the work of Stigler provides our starting-point. His 1964 article in the *Journal of Political Economy* focuses upon firms' attempts to detect price-cutting by rivals. From an analysis of the behaviour of buyers, Stigler concludes that the probability of detection in an industry depends upon market structure. In particular he suggests that it increases with the Herfindahl index of concentration. In other words, then, detection power, and hence R and μ, are all an increasing function of concentration. This is significant for two reasons. First, for its specific conclusion. It shows how we are proposing a structure conduct performance model *within* the environment of collusion. Thus we have argued that the key feature of conduct is collusion and this is present in all industries. However, the consequences of collusion vary and this will be reflected in observed price–cost margins. For instance by putting Stigler (1964) alongside equation (9) we can conclude: concentration (i.e. structure) determines price-cutting (i.e. conduct), and conduct determines price–cost margins (i.e. performance). Second, the Stigler analysis is significant because it shows the more general point that the determinants of R can be explored by looking in more detail at market structure. It is to this that we now turn, bearing in mind that for our purposes here the element of market structure that is particularly interesting is the presence of transnationals, one indication of which is illustrated by our market share data for the UK.

TRANSNATIONALS AND THE DETERMINANTS OF PRICE–COST MARGINS

Firms in general will push the degree of monopoly upwards by influencing the factors we have isolated as its vital determinants. But the presence of transnationals in particular will have a major effect via R.[26]

The clearest indication of this is the reasons for their existence. Firms become transnationals either to consolidate or to improve their retaliatory power – i.e. to defend against or to try to attack rivals. Their attempts at doing so are of course no guarantee of success but in general it is reasonable to rule out mistakes as exceptional and of no real consequence – for our purposes here, that is; if firms believe there is an opportunity to consolidate or improve retaliatory power, we can assume they are right. This is exactly parallel to the way firms can be said to pursue profits – they will sometimes make errors and end up making losses but generally will be successful. Thus (in a comparative static sense)[27] an industry characterised by the presence of transnationals will, other things being equal, tend to have a higher R than an industry where they are absent, because it tends to be characterised by firms with higher levels of retaliatory power.[28]

An alternative and related[29] way of seeing this is to look at the way higher retaliatory power may be suggested by some distinguishing features of transnationals.

One aspect of this is their detection power. Detection not only requires the interpretation of information but also its collection and its being made available to decision-makers. Good internal communication is therefore vital to a firm. An advantage of transnationals in this respect is their appreciation of and experience with modern communication techniques, including methods of organising the firm. This is well documented. Hymer (1972) for instance refers to the importance of organisational form and Vernon (1977) feels that 'The international telephone, the computer and the commercial aircraft have been indispensable to the growth of such enterprises' (p. 1). Similarly Barnet and Muller (1974) tell of IBM's communications network allowing an engineer in a New York laboratory to talk and jointly design circuits with an engineer in Hursley, England, the network permitting the two-way transfer of designs as they work. They also emphasise the importance of centralised management techniques, vital to which is the information flow transnationals develop on a world-wide basis:

> The economic analyst of Ford, for example, whose job in part is to predict when currency devaluations will take place, maintains a complete library on key national officials in the countries where Ford operates, much as the CIA masses similar sorts of data to help in making political predictions. He tries, as he explained to a *Fortune* interviewer, to get 'into the skin of financial bureaucrats' to decide when or whether they will devalue the local currency. He claims to have accurately predicted key currency decisions in 69 out of 75 monetary crises. (p. 36)

This will all help a firm to collect and make available the essential and critical information decision-makers require in retaliating against rivals. They can then act far more quickly and with greater knowledge. In terms of Figure 3.2, then, $\hat{t}$ will tend to be smaller for transnationals.

This outcome is also implied by the especial significance for at least some transnationals of inter-firm collaborative ventures. The world motor vehicles industry is a good case in point; Dicken (1986) reports a maze of inter-firm agreements involving transnationals. He tells of the collaboration between General Motors and Toyota to build a small car in California; of the agreement by which Nissan assembles the Volkswagen Santana in Japan using imported engines, transmissions and suspension but Japanese bodies; of the 'collaborative spider's web' in Europe involving 'virtually all the major European manufacturers'; and so on. The importance of this to detection power is that generally collaborative ventures will enable firms to understand each other all the better.[30] Working together can only help the understanding between General Motors, Toyota, Nissan, Volkswagen and the other motor manufacturers, for instance. The result is that transnationals will build a better picture of which rivals might be more likely to indulge in price-cutting and hence which require close scrutiny. It could be, for example, that certain firms are persistent offenders; for some reason or another they have a tendency to attempt to gain profits at rivals' expense by cutting price.

More generally, greater understanding between firms will also tend to follow from their being rivals in different markets, i.e. from multi-market contacts. This is similar to the case of people; more contact is inclined to lead to more knowledge and understanding. And again transnationals are especially significant in this respect. The reason is that their global activities take them into many markets. For instance Table 3.8 shows the wide geographical distribution of foreign affiliates

Table 3.8: *The geographical distribution of the foreign affiliates of 9481 transnational corporations, 1973*

	Percentage of transnationals with links in				
1 Country	2–5 Countries	6–10 Countries	11–15 Countries	16–20 Countries	>20 Countries
44.9	34.8	10.2	4.4	2.3	3.4

Source: Dicken (1986), and originally the Commission of the European Communities.

of nearly 10,000 transnationals in 1973. Over 30 per cent had affiliates in more than five countries. Moreover the gloss on this general picture is that amongst large transnationals the dispersion is even wider. For example in 1950 approximately a quarter of the largest 180 United States-registered transnationals operated in over five countries but by 1975 this had risen to very nearly all. (See Vernon, 1979.)

Another effect of multi-market contact by transnationals is that it is likely to increase their response power. The basis for this view is an idea associated with Corwin D. Edwards. He argues that when 'powerful enterprises' have reiterated contacts with each other they will decide what to do in one market by bearing in mind their relationship elsewhere. (See Edwards, 1955; 1979). A number of writers have been concerned with this in the context of a given country[31] but it is clearly very relevant to transnationals. Suppose, for example, transnationals A and B produce and sell a particular good in markets X, Y and Z. If firm A contemplates any price-cutting in market X, retaliation from firm B could come from any or all of the markets. One possibility is for B to increase its output in all three, another to use production from Y and Z to swamp market X with vastly increased sales, always assuming there is some freedom of international trade that permits this to happen. In short, then, transnationals have the ability to respond from all or some of the markets in which they operate. This can only increase their response power and hence, other things being equal, only increase R.

This leads to the more general point that transnationals can respond using all of their global resources. For instance, they could finance response in one country by profits from elsewhere, which is undoubtedly important because retaliation by cutting price not only requires more is produced but also that it is produced without bankruptcy. Of course any firm can draw on all of its resources but a distinguishing feature of transnationals is their sheer size. This is again well evidenced. For example Benson and Lloyd (1983) have observed that of the 100 largest economic units in the world, only half are nation-states, the other half are transnationals! And to quote again from Barnet and Muller's *Global Reach*:

If we compare the annual sales of corporations with the gross national produce of countries for 1973, we discover that GM is bigger than Switzerland, Pakistan and South Africa; that Royal Dutch Shell is bigger than Iran, Venezuela, and Turkey; and that Goodyear Tyre is bigger than Saudi Arabia. (p. 15)

Suffice it to say that for most firms, at least, the wrath of such giants would be overwhelming. An industry in which they are present will accordingly tend to have a higher R than otherwise, other things being equal.

TRANSNATIONALS' MARKET SHARE AND MONOPOLISATION IN THE UK

There is plenty to imply that transnationals have a major effect on price–cost margins. One thing that should be very clear from our analysis is that their influence will depend upon various factors – for instance, the way becoming a transnational to improve retaliatory power is actually translated into an improvement, the amount of multi-market contacts, etc. Nevertheless it should be equally clear that if transnationals have a significant presence in an industry, the price–cost margin will tend to be significantly higher, other things being equal. Similarly, if transnationals have a growing significance, price–cost margins will tend to rise ever higher.

Thus in the case of the UK we reported evidence showing that transnationals are important, and increasingly so. We can now see that this suggests the presence of transnationals will lead to significantly higher and ever higher UK price–cost margins. This is only a suggestion and it does not mean that transnationals increase monopolisation in all markets at all times. But in one of the world's major economies they are certainly playing a very prominent role and it at least seems likely that as a result monopolisation is increased and growing. Moreover we saw earlier that movements in price–cost margins can have important welfare implications. In particular increased and growing monopolisation will potentially mean a lower and falling share of income for wages. Hence our conclusion is not something which should be taken lightly; it is potentially very significant.

MATHEMATICAL APPENDIX: A FORMAL STRUCTURE CONDUCT PERFORMANCE MODEL

The typical transnational's price-cost margin is shown in the text as follows:

$$\frac{p - c_t}{p} = \frac{1}{\varepsilon} S_t \frac{dX}{dX_t}$$

(3)

However,

$$\frac{dX}{dX_t} = 1 + \sum_{j \neq t}^{T} \frac{dX_j}{dX_t} + \sum_{n=1}^{N} \frac{dX_n}{dX_t},$$

where n is the typical firm only producing in one country. Moreover define:

$$a \equiv \frac{dX_j}{dX_t} \frac{X_t}{X_j} \forall t, j = 1, 2, \ldots T; \ t \neq j$$

Then:

$$\sum_{j \neq t} \frac{dX_j}{dX_t} = \sum_{j \neq t} a \frac{X_j}{X_t} = a \sum_{j \neq t} \frac{X_j}{X_t} = a \left(\frac{1}{\hat{S}_t} - 1 \right)$$

where

$$\hat{S}_t \equiv \frac{X_t}{X_T}, \ X_T \equiv \sum_{t=1}^{T}{}_{|t}.$$

Similarly,

$$\beta \equiv \frac{dX_n}{dX_t} \frac{X_t}{X_n} \forall n = 1, 2, \ldots N; \ t = 1, 2, \ldots T$$

$$\Rightarrow \sum_{n=1}^{N} \frac{dX_n}{dX_t} = \beta \left(\frac{1}{S_t} - \frac{1}{\hat{S}_t} \right)$$

where: $S_t \equiv \dfrac{X_t}{X}$. Substituting into the price-cost margin expression yields:

$$\frac{p - c_t}{p} = \frac{1}{\varepsilon} S_t \left[1 + a\left(\frac{1}{S_t} - 1\right) + \beta\left(\frac{1}{S_t} - \frac{1}{\tilde{S_t}}\right) \right]$$

$$\Rightarrow \frac{p - c_t}{p} = \frac{1}{\varepsilon}\left[S_t + a(S_T - S_t) + \beta(1 - S_T) \right]$$

where $S_T \equiv \dfrac{X_T}{X}$. Rearranging:

$$\frac{p - c_t}{p} = \frac{1}{\varepsilon}[\beta + (a - \beta)S_T + (1 - a)S_t] \tag{4}$$

Consider now the typical national corporation, firm n. Similarly to the above

$$\frac{p - c_n}{p} = \frac{1}{\varepsilon} S_n \frac{dX}{dX_n}$$

and

$$\frac{dX}{dX_n} = 1 + \sum_{k \neq n}^{N} \frac{dX_k}{dX_n} + \sum_{t=1}^{T} \frac{dX_t}{dX_n}$$

Defining $\sigma \equiv \dfrac{dX_k}{dX_n}\dfrac{X_n}{X_k} \; \forall n, k = 1, 2, \ldots N, k \neq n$

and $\gamma \equiv \dfrac{dX_t}{dX_n}\dfrac{X_n}{X_t} \; \forall n = 1, 2, \ldots N$ and $t = 1, 2, \ldots T$, then:

$$\frac{p - c_n}{p} = \frac{1}{\varepsilon}\left[S_n + \sigma(S_N - S_n) + \gamma(1 - S_N) \right]$$

where $S_n \equiv \dfrac{X_n}{X}$ and $S_N = \displaystyle\sum_{n=1}^{N} S_n$. Thus, assuming $a = \gamma$ and $\beta = \sigma$ and given $S_N + S_T = 1$, this yields:

$$\frac{p - c_n}{p} = \frac{1}{\varepsilon}\left[\beta + (a + \beta)S_T + (1 - \beta)S_n\right] \tag{5}$$

Multiplying (4) by S_t, (5) by S_n and summing over all firms gives a weighted average price-cost margin:

$$\mu \equiv \sum_{i=1}^{N+T} \frac{p - c_i}{p} \frac{X_i}{X} = \frac{1}{\varepsilon}\left\{\left[\beta + (a - \beta)S_T\right]\sum_{t=1}^{T} S_t + (1 - a)\sum_{t=1}^{T} S_t^2 + \right.$$

$$\left. \left[\beta + (a - \beta)S_T\right]\sum_{n=1}^{N} S_n + (1 - \beta)\sum_{n=1}^{N} S_n^2\right\}$$

$$= \frac{1}{\varepsilon}\left\{\beta + (a - \beta)S_T + (1 - a)\sum_{t=1}^{T} S_t^2 + (1 - \beta)\sum_{n=1}^{N} S_n^2\right\}$$

However:

$$\sum_{t=1}^{T} S_t^2 = S_T^2 H_T; \quad \sum_{n=1}^{N} S_n^2 = S_N^2 H_N$$

where: $H_T \equiv \displaystyle\sum_{t=1}^{T} \hat{S}_t^2$, the Herfindahl concentration index amongst transnationals; $H_N \equiv \displaystyle\sum_{n=1}^{N} \hat{S}_n^2$, the Herfindahl concentration index amongst national corporations. Also, the Herfindahl for the whole industry is given by the following:

$$H = S_T^2 H_T + S_N^2 H_N$$

Thus by substitution:

$$(1-a) \sum_{t=1}^{T} S_t^2 + (1-\beta) \sum_{n=1}^{N} S_n^2 = (1-a)S_T^2 H_T + (1-\beta)S_N^2 H_N$$

$$= (1-a)S_T^2 H_T + (1-\beta)(H - S_T^2 H_T)$$

$$= (1-\beta)H + S_T^2 H_T (1-a-1+\beta)$$

$$= (1-\beta)H - (a-\beta)S_T^2 H_T$$

Substituting this into the expression for u:

$$\mu \equiv \frac{1}{\varepsilon} \quad \{\beta + (a-\beta)S_T + (1-\beta)H - (a-\beta)S^2{}_T H_T\}$$

In other words,

$$\mu = \frac{\beta}{\varepsilon} + \frac{(1-\beta)}{\varepsilon}H + \frac{(a-\beta)(1-S_T H_T)S_T}{\varepsilon} \tag{6}$$

STATISTICAL APPENDIX: FIRMS INCLUDED IN THE SALES AND EMPLOYMENT ESTIMATES FOR LEADING UK TRANSNATIONALS, BY INDUSTRY

Principal industry	Firm	Included in sales estimates*	Included in employment estimates*
Aerospace	British Aerospace plc		√
Building products	Consolidated Gold Fields plc		√
	Pilkington Brothers plc	√	√
	RMC Group plc		√
	Thomas Tilling plc	√	√
	Turner & Newall Ltd		√
Drink	Bass plc		√
Electrical engineering and electronics	BICC plc	√	√
	The General Electric Co plc	√	√
	The Plessey Co plc		√
	Thorn EMI plc	√	
Food	Associated British Foods Ltd	√	√
	Brooke Bond Group plc		√
	Cadbury Schweppes plc	√	√
	Hanson Trust plc	√	√
	Rank Hovis McDougall plc	√	√
	Rowntree Mackintosh plc	√	√
	Tate and Lyle plc	√	√
	Unigate Ltd	√	√
	United Biscuits (Holdings) Ltd	√	√
Health products and consumer chemicals	Beecham Group plc	√	√
	Glaxo Holdings plc		√
	Reckitt & Colman plc	√	√
Industrial and agricultural chemicals	BOC Group plc		√
	Imperial Chemical Industries plc		√
Industrial and farm equipment	Babcock International plc	√	√
	Hawker Siddeley Group plc	√	√

Metals and metal products	British Steel Corporation plc		✓
	IMI plc	✓	✓
	Johnson Matthey & Co Ltd	✓	✓
	Metal Box plc	✓	✓
	Rio Tinto Zinc Corporation Ltd	✓	✓
	TI Group plc	✓	✓
Motor vehicles	BL plc	✓	✓
	Guest Keen & Nettlefold plc	✓	✓
	Lucas Industries plc	✓	✓
Paper and wood products	The Bowater Corporation plc		✓
	Reed International plc	✓	✓
Petroleum products	British Petroleum Co plc		✓
	The Burmah Oil plc		✓
	Royal Dutch/Shell Group of Companies		✓
	Ultramar plc		✓
Rubber	Dunlop Holdings Ltd		✓
Textiles, clothing, footwear	Coates Paton plc	✓	✓
	Courtaulds plc	✓	
Tobacco	Imperial Group plc		✓
	Rothmans International Ltd		✓

*Inclusion is signified by a ✓.

NOTES

1. As regards our aims in this chapter, at least.

2. $\mu = \dfrac{\Pi + F}{V} \Rightarrow \dfrac{\Pi + F}{Y} = \mu\dfrac{V}{Y}; \dfrac{\Pi + F}{Y} = \mu\dfrac{V}{Y} \Rightarrow$

$$\dfrac{Y - W}{Y} = \mu\dfrac{V}{Y} \Rightarrow \dfrac{W}{Y} = l - \mu\dfrac{V}{Y}.$$

3. See also the analysis of wage shares in Cowling and Molho (1982), where this point is discussed.

4. Although not vast this has concentrated on the effects on transnationals *vis-à-vis* other profitability measures (see for instance the survey in Caves (1982), Gaspari (1983) and Dunning (1985)).
5. See also the evidence in United Nations (1983).
6. 'Foreign enterprises are those controlled or owned by companies incorporated overseas', *Business Monitor PA 1002* (1981), p. 20. 'Controlled', for practical purposes, means a majority shareholding. It does not necessarily mean this simply because non-limited companies are included in the Census of Production and so control other than by shareholding is possible. However the number of non-limited companies is of minor importance and they can effectively be ignored.
7. Stopford (1982), p. xii. Given our focus on manufacturing, the reference to mining may appear disturbing. However it is not so much of a problem when it is realised that, from 1980, the UK Census of Production includes mining activity in manufacturing. Note also that Stopford (1982) excludes 'firms in banking, insurance, commodity broking, retailing, engineering contracting and other service industries' (p. xii).
8. Sales are estimated from information on (a) total net sales and (b) the percentage of those sales by foreign subsidiaries and by UK exports. On some occasions (a) is affected by intra-firm trade; e.g. the figure for GEC in 1981 includes £258 million of intra-firm trade. Sometimes (b) is affected – e.g. for Courtaulds.
9. The accounting basis is that used in Stopford (1982) and not Stopford, Dunning and Haberich (1980). Thus, for instance, any company account ending between 31 March 1977 and 30 March 1978 is included in the 1977 estimates.
10. Assuming a (and β) is the same for transnationals and national corporations is another mere simplifier leaving our conclusions unaffected.

11. $$\frac{dp}{dX_t} = \frac{dp}{dX}\frac{dX}{dX_t} = \frac{dp}{dX}\left(1 + \sum_{j \neq t}\frac{dX_j}{dX_t}\right)$$

The dX_j/dX_t terms are conjectural variations. An alternative is to express these conjectures using elasticities, as in the Mathematical Appendix.

12. See for example Sawyer (1979).
13. (i) Another response has recently been the consistent conjectures approach (see for instance Bresnahan (1981), Perry (1982), Boyer and Moreaux (1983), Kamien and Schwartz (1983) and Ulph (1983)). This requires that firm i's conjecture coincides with the way its rival in fact reacts. However it is very restrictive because other factors need to be analysed to verify whether or not conclusions are valid. For example Kamien and Schwartz (1983) require symmetric duopolists facing a linear market demand function to price at marginal cost. This must be wrong. For instance ignoring legal constraints – reasonable in the context of these theoretical models – it is undoubtedly *possible* for such firms to formally agree to maximise joint profits.

(ii) Clarke (1982) has also argued that to allege a contradiction is to miss the point. Whilst a conjecture shown to be wrong appears myopic it is actually in the combined interests of firms to adopt such conjectures as they will thereby increase joint profits. However, then the crucial question is: why should firms seek to increase combined profits? In short, it is again left unexplained why a situation arises.

14. First-order conditions such as equation (2) have been used to deny a causal link between structure and performance (see for instance Clarke and Davies (1982)). The argument is that in first-order conditions market shares are endogenous and cannot be determinants of price-cost margins; rather they are simultaneously determined *with* price–cost margins. In the context of the formal model and ignoring the Fellner and Stigler contradiction, this is correct. But this does not mean structure is never a causal factor; for instance a different model could be set up where current conduct is a function of past market structure. Thus no real conceptual issues are being confronted. Moreover the contradiction cannot be ignored and, as we have seen, removing it means that the formal model does not tackle determinants anyway.

15. This is not what many other authors mean by collusion. For instance Waterson (1984) p. 23 takes the typical view that collusion refers to implicit or explicit joint profit-maximisation amongst firms.

16. Albeit not a major problem; industries are typically dominated in practice by a few giant firms.

17. Se also Phillips (1962), who points out that: 'Interdependence may involve but a few firms or it may include thousands' (p. 29).

18. Scherer (1980) disagrees with this view but does not give a reason.

19. In practice there will always be uncertainty because of, for instance, costs of acquiring information.

20. Cowling and Sugden (1986) discusses this in more detail in the context of an analysis of exchange rate adjustments and European car prices.

21. Because firm i's price cut attracts buyers from rivals, rivals' profits must decline for as long as they make no response.

22. That they are at most only simplifiers is explained as follows. Relaxing the certainty assumption (c) merely requires talk of expected changes in profits. Assumption (a) simply confines attention to one price response; realistically there may be more but this only introduces more twists and turns into Figure 3.2. Assumption (b) is realistic – firms do have finite planning horizons. Assumption (d) means that changed prices yield immediately changed profits – relaxation simply requires learning and hence gradual profit changes.

23. $\dfrac{\delta \Delta \Pi_i}{\delta \hat{t}} = \Pi_2 - \Pi_1 - (\Pi_3 - \Pi_1) = \Pi_2 - \Pi_3 > 0. \ \dfrac{\delta \Delta \Pi_i}{\delta \Pi_3} = \hat{T} - \hat{t} > 0$

24. It is worth pointing out that collectively firms can agree on measures which improve their detection powers. For example they could publish their trading prices, or use more sophisticated devices such as sales contract clauses which allow a seller to meet any lower prices a buyer

may be offered (see Salop (1982)). As regards response power, its very essence is a game of bluff and counter-bluff. More generally, see Scherer (1980).

25. This is not to deny that there are other influences in Figure 3.2/equation (8). Our aim is simply to focus on the crucial aspects. Note also that we have been silent on entry. This allows concentration on different aspects of monopolisation. In any case entry will not pose major problems. It could be analysed within the same sort of framework and, as Cowling (1982) argues, appropriate responses to it will generally not impact on price–cost margins. See also the critical survey of the entry literature in Encaoua, Geroski and Jacquemin (1982).

26. See Cowling (1982) for a discussion of firms' influence on ε. Also interesting here is the view that transnationals arise because a firm producing a good where it is marketed can better adapt it to local tastes (see Vernon (1966), Caves (1971) and Macewan (1972)). The adaptation can be seen as obtaining a less elastic demand.

27. If an industry is initially in a situation where no firm is changing its output but then a firm acquires additional retaliatory power, the initial stability will be upset. Quite how this leads to a new stable situation is not relevant to our argument here in so far as we are simply focusing upon equation (9) in a comparative static framework.

28. (i) Note also how this means that firms becoming transnationals can effect R, hence price–cost margins and, following our introductory comments, can potentially alter the functional distribution of income. This underlines how our analysis in Chapter 2 (of why transnationals come into existence) centres on distribution rather than efficiency. (ii) There is also a possibility of an indirect effect on R via concentration. If firms becoming transnationals can sufficiently improve their retaliatory power they may be able, for instance, to drive rivals out of the market. This will alter concentration and therefore influence R via the detection effects contemplated by Stigler (1964).

29. It is related because a transnational's features are a product of why it arises.

30. They could also provide an institutional framework for successful collusion.

31. See for instance Bulow, Geanakoplos and Klemperer (1985), and the empirical analyses of the US in Scott (1982) and Feinberg (1985).

4 The Rise of Transnationals and the International Division of Labour

In Chapter 2 we laid down a framework which sees firms becoming transnational either because of the risks which lead them to defend against rivals, or because of the advantages which cause them to attack. The vital underlying concept at the heart of this analysis is retaliatory power, explored in Chapter 3 *vis-à-vis* the impact on price–cost margins. Our aim now is to move on from this by exploring a specific reason for the existence of transnationals that takes us into an examination of labour markets.

A potentially important determinant of these risks, advantages and hence retaliatory power is a lower labour cost. This may enable a firm to undercut a rival's price and gain profits at a rival's expense; a lower price attracts buyers from rivals and the lower a firm's costs the lower it can drop its price without making fatal losses, other things being equal. A firm may therefore defend itself against the risk that rivals obtain lower labour costs. Similarly, a firm may attack rivals by seeking lower labour costs for itself. One way to argue that this will lead to transnationals is to use the traditional comparative cost advantage theory. This says that costs of different types of labour vary across countries and that firms will take opportunity of this by producing wherever it is cheapest (see for instance the survey in Koutsoyiannis (1982)). But this is far too restrictive because it sees firms as passive reactors to given cost conditions. In fact, costs depend upon the bargaining power of labour and its employers and this is endogenous to firms' decisions, a point discussed fairly extensively in a line of literature looking at the domestic scene (see for example Marglin (1974) on the introduction of factories, Edwards (1979a) on hierarchy in the workplace, and the reviews of McPherson (1983) and Marginson (1986)).

Accordingly we shall follow this line of literature in our analysis. In particular we shall argue that an important reason why transnationals arise is 'divide and rule': by producing in various countries firms divide their workforce, thereby reduce labour's bargaining power, and consequently obtain lower labour costs.

We shall first explore this in a theoretical analysis and subsequently look at some empirics. The theory is implicit in such existing works as Fröbel, Heinrichs and Kreye, *The New International Division of Labour* (1980). It is nevertheless worth doing because it attempts to add to these works, which neither go into the same detail nor are in the context of the framework of Chapter 2 (and Chapter 3). As for the empirics, they try to establish divide and rule as an at least contributory reason for the existence of some transnationals. This is obviously limited in so far as it does not attempt to establish its exact influence. Yet it is a valid and useful beginning because many are very quick to dismiss the explanation on the basis of allegedly widespread evidence that transnationals pay wages at least as high as their rivals'. Such a dismissal is simply not based on the facts.

A THEORETICAL ANALYSIS OF 'DIVIDE AND RULE' AND TRANSNATIONALS

A firm's labour costs depend upon such factors as wage rates, the effort workers put into their assigned tasks, the time they are allowed for tea breaks, and so on. There is a conflict over these costs in so far as employers and workers will have different optima. This can be seen very clearly in the case of wage rates, for example;[1] with all else being the same – and this includes having a job! – a worker will prefer higher wages than his or her employer. In a perfect labour market this conflict is resolved by competition. For instance any attempt by employers to depress wage rates and thereby increase their profits would be met by other firms entering the market, paying higher wages and obtaining normal returns. However, this is an unrealistic scenario that can be confined to theoretical daydreaming. For example, similar to the way firms will collude over prices to avoid merely normal profits, should it be necessary they will collude over wages to avoid competition that leaves them all worse off.[2] Moreover when there are plenty of workers to go round, collusion will tend to be unnecessary, and we have already emphasised that the world we are depicting has a tendency towards unemployment. In practice, then, the concept of a perfect labour market is a red herring. What actually happens in the real world is that the outcome of their conflict is determined by the bargaining power of workers and employers.

In its turn bargaining power depends very much on the ability of workers to act collectively. (See Burkitt and Bowers (1979) for instance.)[3] If they do not act together workers tend to have a weaker bargaining position. This results from various factors, such as:

(a) it allows employers to replace specific workers by re-arranging the activities of others, thereby offsetting any loss that may result from failure to settle the conflict;[4]
(b) it increases worker competition for jobs, greater competition implying a weaker bargaining position; and
(c) it reduces the information workers have of their value to particular employers.

Moreover the significance of this to us is that collective action is, at least, very difficult when people work in different countries.

The reasons for this are manifest and well documented (see e.g. Gennard (1972), Craypo (1975), Ullman (1975), ILO (1976), Northrup (1978), Kujawa (1979, 1979a), Helfgott (1983)).[5] They include such organisational problems as devising the institutional arrangements for international trade unions but also more deep-rooted cultural factors such as different languages, xenophobia and different religions. For

instance CIS (1978) talks of the problems faced by Ford
workers in Europe, let alone the world:

It's difficult enough for Ford workers in one country, sharing a common
language and separated by comparatively small distances, to organise
effectively against the company on anything more than a local plant or shop
level. Even here, major problems of communication, sectionalism, and
cumbersome national union machinery arise. On a European scale the
problems are multiplied many times. Workers in France, Germany, Bel-
gium, Spain and the UK use six different languages plus those of the
immigrants. It means much greater distances – over a thousand miles from
Halewood to Valencia, with disproportionately large travel and telephone
costs as a result. There are that many more unions – and another layer, the
international union organisation, on top. (p.30)

In principle it should be possible to overcome the purely
organisational problems without too much difficulty. After
all, transnational corporations provide an indication of how
activities can be organised where large distances are involved.
But fundamental problems are posed by the cultural factors
and these at least have no easy solution. Indeed, they reveal a
basic asymmetry between labour and its employers at the
world level. Whereas collective action by labour requires a
considerable amount of cooperation between different
workers, employers have nowhere near as many problems.
First, they are not so different because they talk a common
language, have a common love and a common religion: profit.
But also, pursuing profits across the globe does not require the
same level of cooperation by people from different countries
that would be demanded of workers should they act collectively; rather, it merely requires appropriate hierarchical organisations into which people can be slotted. This is more a
problem of coordination than of cooperation.

All this clearly suggests that a firm may decide to produce in
various countries so that it can face a more fragmented
workforce. Put another way, a reason for transnationals to
exist is because firms producing in various countries divide
their workforce, thereby reducing labour's bargaining power,
and consequently obtaining lower labour costs.[6]

To illustrate, suppose a firm manufactures shirts in two
stages: cutting and then the sewing of cloth. Assume that
initially all of its manufacturing facilities are in the UK and

that its workforce is united, quick to seize the opportunity to act collectively to maintain working conditions. For example if the firm tries to reduce the tea breaks enjoyed by its cutters the workers are all prepared to strike, completely halting production. The firm can respond to this in various ways. One possibility is to transfer part of both its cutting and sewing operations to, say, the Philippines. Then, even if its UK workers have a grievance which leads them to strike, while work continues in the Philippines the firm can indefinitely maintain at least partial supply to its customers.[7] A second option is to divide its workforce by transferring the sewing operation to the Philippines. A case when this might be preferable is if it doubts the skill of Philippino workers to do the cutting, because it will still reduce workers' bargaining power in certain circumstances. For instance, if it now tries to reduce cutters' tea breaks, production will not stop as long as there are stocks of cut cloth to supply Philippino sewers and those sewers are willing to work.[8]

This is not to deny that even without transferring any production outside of the UK the firm could undermine strikes. For example it could build up stocks of finished goods to enable supplies to customers to continue at least for a while. But the critical point is that the possibilities for reducing labour's bargaining power by producing in various countries gives added degrees of freedom – more room to manoeuvre. Nor are the possibilities of transferring operations to the Philippines the firm's only options. It has many others. For instance it could transfer activity to somewhere other than the Philippines; or divide its workforce amongst three, four, five or even more countries. The choice it makes will thus depend upon many factors: the skill of workers in one part of the world versus the skill of those elsewhere; its expectations of worker 'militancy' in Europe as compared to Asia; and so on. Worthy of special recognition, however, are the significance of the role of nation-states and the choice of organisational form.

Nation-states are important for two reasons. First, they can directly influence labour costs, for instance by such obvious means as legislation affecting working hours, the right to strike, etc., but also by more subtle ways such as propaganda encouraging greater effort from workers. Thus the choice between locating in the Philippines and the UK will be influenced by the policies adopted by the two nation-states. Secondly, the actions of nation-states are not independent of the wishes of firms; i.e. these too are endogenous to firms' activities. The exact relationship between states and firms is controversial[9] but it is clear that whatever it is, firms can in fact be seen bargaining with nation-states for legislation, etc. that they find desirable.[10] Both of these points are suggested by Fröbel *et al.*'s (1980) discussion of the acquisition by Nino AG, a West German textile producer, of production facilities in Wexford, Ireland. The views of Eire's development agency chairman are quoted from the economic supplement of the West German newspaper *Frankfurter Allgemeine Zeitung*:

> You have heard that this German company wishes to extend its operations here in Wexford. . . . However, the plans for this expansion do not only depend on the state of the economy, but also on how much you people here in Wexford are willing to co-operate with this undertaking . . . you should . . . bear in mind that we are competing with many other countries in the world to obtain new industries, and that there are development corporations everywhere. We therefore have to convince the investor that he is going to find himself in surroundings which will let him succeed. (p. 122)

On the one hand this tells of a state official encouraging workers to give more to the firm and on the other hand it recognises competition between countries and the willingness by a firm to exploit this – the point being made, that the Irish have to compete with others seeking investors.

The significance of organisational form to firms becoming transnationals was recognised in general by Hymer (1972). Using the US as an illustration, he noted the growth of 'Marshallian type, single-function firms' into large corporations requiring completely different forms of organisation, especially the so-called multidivisional form.[11] He argues that this helped to provide 'the power to go abroad' because it gave firms an appropriate administrative structure.[12] However, with the more specific issue of divide and rule leading to transnationals, the choice between market and non-market exchanges is especially interesting.

Our preferred view is that a firm is the means of coordinating production from one centre of strategic decision-making and that this coordination can include both market and non-market exchanges. Thus suppose our shirt manufacturer decides to respond to a militant workforce by dividing its sewing operations between the Philippines and the UK. One possibility is simply to set up factories in both countries and have nothing to do with the market until the final goods are sold to the consumers. Another may be to subcontract the sewing to small workshops dotted throughout the UK and the Philippines. This would involve market exchanges because the workshops would be contracted to do some sewing in consideration for a specified sum of money. But provided production was being coordinated from one centre of strategic decision-making, there would still be only one firm.[13] Moreover the subcontracting option may be particularly appealing to a firm because it can provide an extreme division of a militant workforce. For instance whilst those Ford workers employed in huge plants clearly identified with the Ford Motor Company find organising collective action very difficult, imagine the problems of workers dotted across the world in small workshops operating under completely different names. How many would even begin to recognise that they work for the same firm? Simply attempting to organise collective action would be a nightmare. Actually doing so would verge on the impossible.

Having said this a firm will not necessarily use the subcontracting option. It may be impossible because of limitations in available technology; some production activity – for example, in manufacturing cars – cannot be carried out in small workshops. Furthermore it may be simply unnecessary, for example because workers can be broken into a very weak body with no real bargaining power without resort to such extreme division. It may be sufficient to locate one plant in the Philippines, another in the UK and rely on (or perhaps promote)[14] racial tension to keep UK and Philippino workers completely alienated.

A critical welfare implication of this divide-and-rule analysis is yet again distributional. This is partly because it sits within the framework and alongside the analysis that we have developed in earlier chapters. Thus from Chapter 2 it should be clear that when divide and rule is a basis for a firm becoming a transnational it may result in redundancies and hence unemployment.[15] And from our discussion in Chapter 3 it should be clear that the divide-and-rule strategy may lead to a reduction in the share of income going to wages – via decreased labour costs implying increased retaliatory power and therefore a higher degree of monopoly. But in addition the distributional implications are partly because distribution is the very essence of the bargaining analysis. The whole point is that a firm produces in different countries to weaken its workers' bargaining power and thereby to increase profits at the expense of those workers. Thus even ignoring the unemployment and wage-share aspects, our divide-and-rule analysis has vital implications for distribution. Of course workers are likely to realise this. They will therefore attempt to prevent a firm producing in various countries by agreeing to lower labour costs if it will produce in just one, albeit not so low as if it were a transnational. This may appeal to a firm if it can thereby avoid any extra costs that result from producing in various countries – e.g. what the Hymer (1960)/Kindleberger (1969) approach calls 'costs of operating at a distance'.[16] It will also leave the workers better off. For instance the workers of the shirt manufacturer initially producing solely in the UK but contemplating production in other countries will temper their militancy to prevent this happening. Thus they will try to maintain as high a level of utility as possible. However, transnationals will still arise in some situations if for no other reason than the fact that bargaining is by its very nature a game of bluff and counter-bluff. For instance workers may not believe the need to accept lower wages to prevent a firm becoming a transnational, yet if they call their employer's bluff and are shown to be wrong, a transnational will arise. Or perhaps a firm does not believe its workers' claim that if it produced in various countries tea breaks could not be profitably cut; it would then call its workers' bluff and become a transnational.[17]

A further implication concerns the international division of labour. Divide and rule leading to transnationals results in a firm's manufacturing operations being spread across different countries. The exact locations will depend upon the factors we have mentioned but there is nothing to limit the spread encompassing the whole world. Whilst those parts of the production process requiring skilled labour will tend to be focused on the old industrialised countries of the western world, unskilled activity knows no bounds. Moreover techno-logical change is endogenous to the wishes of firms; they will seek the production technology they find most desirable (see Marglin (1974)). Thus over time they can look for technology which deskills all operations. The benefits of divide and rule *vis-à-vis* profits will give an incentive to do this, thereby opening the entire world to more and more of their manufac-turing activities.

In short, then, our analysis leads to the so-called 'new international division of labour' that has been widely evi-denced and discussed in the likes of Hymer (1972), Adam (1975), Fröbel *et al.* (1980), and more recently in the survey by Dicken (1986). The 'old' division saw the world split into industrial countries and primary producers, international trade being carried out between the two. The industrial countries would buy raw materials and agricultural products from the primary producers, who in return provided a limited market for manufactured goods. However, the new division cuts through this simple dichotomy. Nowadays manufactur-ing is observed throughout the world. Thus whereas the traditional manufacturing nations have been in relative, even absolute, decline, the 'newly industrialising countries' have grown very rapidly. Dicken (1986) for instance notes that 'the centre of gravity of the world manufacturing system' has begun to shift from North America and Western Europe to the Pacific.

Having said this it is also very important to realise that our analysis does not imply any shift in strategic decision-making. This is significant because strategic decisions – which include where to locate manufacturing – determine the direction of a firm. They are therefore crucial.[18] But divide and rule merely leads to locating manufacturing throughout the world and is no reason for strategic decision-makers to move as well. Traditionally they have been located in the large cities of the major industrialised nations. There is no reason for this to

change. An office in New York, London, Paris, Frankfurt or
Tokyo has all that they need and yet permits close contact
with their empires, each other, and influential nation-states.
(See again the similar analysis in Hymer 1972.)[19] Indeed in
practice the evidence in Dicken (1986) suggests this has not
changed. In other words, the world we are depicting is
characterised by firms with a global spread of manufacturing
but which are nevertheless controlled from a handful of
locations.

SOME EMPIRICAL EVIDENCE ON 'DIVIDE AND RULE' AND TRANSNATIONALS

A usual reaction to the divide-and-rule hypothesis is to reject
it on the basis of evidence on wage levels in different types of
firm. The argument is that transnationals appear to pay wages
at least as high as their rivals and they therefore cannot be
founded on a division of the workforce to lower labour costs.
The apparent evidence for this comes from many studies
covering many countries.[20] Typical is the analysis in Buckley
and Enderwick (1983) and Blanchflower (1984). This examines senior managements' estimates of employees' average
weekly gross pay in British manufacturing plants using data
from the 1980 *Workplace Industrial Relations Survey*. The
conclusion is that, in general, non-UK-owned plants offer
comparable or higher wages than UK-owned plants. But no
way can this be evidence against divide and rule.

First, there is not even a distinction between transnationals
and their rivals. Correspondingly there is no relevant evidence
of relative wages. The difficulties here are parallel to those we
encountered in Chapter 3 when looking for evidence of
transnationals' market share in UK product markets. Problems arise from the definition of a transnational; reference to
plant ownership does not and cannot distinguish the different
types of firm we are interested in. Rather, control is the key
concept. For instance the activities of foreign-registered transnationals are not confined to non-UK-owned plants. What is
likely to be especially important here is the absence of
subcontracting arrangements, which we have already argued

is significant to the divide-and-rule approach. Moreover the problems also arise because clearly a UK-owned plant could be as much a part of a transnational as a non-UK-owned plant; the distinction therefore fails to pick out transnationals. Thus if UK-owned transnationals are particularly successful at dividing their workforce across the world, they can pay sufficiently low wages to allow non-UK-owned plants to pay more than UK-owned plants whilst transnationals pay less than their rivals.

Secondly, even where transnationals do pay more they may nevertheless be founded upon the divide-and-rule concept. Maintaining the focus on wages this is best seen by an illustration. Suppose firm A is a wage leader in country Y and that it acquires production facilities in country X. It is perfectly feasible for A to be a high payer in X – for example because it feels high wages will attract better workers – yet still pay less than if it produced solely in Y facing a workforce acting collectively. For instance it could still undermine worker bargaining power in Y by diverting production from X to bypass a strike. Moreover this is all consistent with its remaining a wage leader in country Y – for instance, because it continues to face the best organised workers in Y, albeit workers who now have less bargaining power than before. In short, then, a firm can produce in two countries and be a high payer in both, even though the basis of its transnational production is divide and rule.

Furthermore even more important is the fact that wages must only be a part of the story. This is fatal to any claim that wages evidence refutes the divide-and-rule hypothesis; quite simply, the hypothesis centres on labour *costs* and therefore includes many other factors. Forget the wages transnationals pay – what about the effort workers have to put into their jobs,[21] the time they are allowed for lunches, the conditions in which they work, and so on? Even if transnationals do pay higher wages than their rivals it is undoubtedly clear that their labour costs may nevertheless be lower.[22]

To argue successfully that divide and rule is an important reason for the existence of transnationals, however, we must be more positive. It is not enough simply to refute the wages view because this only removes an obstacle from our path.

What is needed is evidence that goes to the heart of the hypothesis, something which wage analysis is incapable of doing. One source of this is the view of participants in firms.

Thus strongly suggestive are the views of the trade unionists summarised by ILO (1976). It refers to 'union concerns' that transnationals 'deliberately' dual source at least some of their activities – i.e. establish alternative sources of supply – so that they can 'thereby reduce the impact of a strike in any one country' (p.20). More generally it also comments that:

One of the most serious charges which unions make, from time to time *vis-à-vis* [transnationals] is that the latter *use their internationally-spread facilities as a threat to counter union demands and power*. If the union will not yield the company can or will threaten to transfer its production to another country, or the company may utilise already existing facilities in another country to penalise the 'demanding' union, or the company may threaten to curtail its future investments in the country in which the union is making 'unreasonable' (in the company's judgment) demands. All of these tactics are subsumed by the unions under the general head of threats to shift production as part of the labour tactics of multinational enterprises. (p.19; emphasis added)[23]

This is supported by 'typical' views from various European unions. Thus the British Trades Union Congress feels that:

In many companies the existence of alternative sources of supply gives management scope to threaten to switch products to other locations. *This can be a very effective bargaining counter.* (Emphasis added)[24]

Similarly the Swedish Metalworkers Union:

Multinational companies have wide opportunities of moving their capital from one company to another. *This . . . makes it more difficult for trade union organisations to pursue their demands* for higher wages, employment and workers' influence in the firms. (Emphasis added)[25]

And an official of the International Metalworkers' Federation has some interesting comments to make:

'*How effectively can we bargain when we only represent 4 per cent of the company's employees?*' That is the question that was put to us at our ITT workers' world meeting last year by the president of the American bakers' union, which represents the workers of ITT's Continental Baking. Of course, this same question is apparent to trade unionists representing workers in the smaller subsidiaries of major multinationals all over the world. Even the powerful unions that represent Vauxhall and Chrysler workers in Great Britain know that they only speak for about 5 per cent in the first case, and a bit of 10 per cent in the second case, of the companies' world workforce. (Emphasis added)[26]

In so far as these views are representative they certainly imply that firms do use the divide-and-rule tactic.

These conclusions are also supported by Greer and Shearer's (1981) survey of US unions.[27] A third of the (six) unions reporting on the issues claim that firms actually use foreign production to undercut the bargaining position of US unions and actually undermine US strikes using foreign production. Particularly interesting and clear-cut is the claim from two (out of seven) unions that firms strengthen their US bargaining position by moving their production or making new investments abroad.

Of course, it is possible that this is all in the imagination of trade unionists. But in the first place the chances of that are slim simply because it is so unlikely that there would be so much smoke without any fire. Moreover, even firms are willing to admit their use of divide-and-rule tactics. Agreed there is no widespread evidence of this but the remarkable thing is that there is any at all. Transnationals seem to be very sensitive to adverse publicity and accordingly use of divide-and-rule tactics is hardly something they will wish to advertise (see ILO (1976)). Yet Greer and Shearer (1981) report a survey of US companies, each non-US-owned.[28] Seven out of 26 firms reporting on the issue agreed they would consider using production in various countries to discourage US strikes. One out of 28 said that it had actually done so. This is also supported by ILO's (1976) reference to the Chrysler Corporation Chairman extolling the benefits of dual sourcing *vis-à-vis* bargaining power. In other words, then, even firms agree that trade unionists are not paranoid in their views of firms' activities – at least, not paranoid all of the time.

The implication from all of this is that divide and rule does indeed lead to the presence of transnationals. The evidence certainly goes to the heart of the matter because it literally asks participants on either side of the labour cost conflict what they think is happening. Trade unionists seem in little doubt.

But they are even joined by some firms (albeit a minority).

For those who remain sceptical there is also the evidence of specific situations. This is very sparse because unfortunately there is again the problem of firms not wishing to advertise their activities. Nevertheless instances are discussed in the literature at odd times. For example, ILO (1976) mentions the case of labour unrest in the UK leading the Chrysler Corporation to contemplate the transfer of production to sister operations in France and/or Japan, and Gennard (1972) the antics of the Goodyear Tyre Company in using supplies from elsewhere to undermine industrial action in Britain. Moreover the activities of Ford have been comparatively well documented.

Thus the clearest possible case of divide and rule is provided by the CIS (1978) report of Ford's decision to deliberately dual source components for its Fiesta model to reduce worker bargaining power. This is shown by its engines policy:

In the event of a shutdown of the Dagenham Fiesta engine line, the company's aim would be to boost output of the Valencia engine line to supply extra units to the Dagenham and Saarlouis assembly lines. With a higher output of the Valencia engined cars from these two plants, stocks of the Dagenham engines could be stretched out to minimise interruptions in supply of any model. Similarly, if the Valencia engine plant were shut down. (p.30)[29]

More subtle is the continuous barrage of threats Ford has hurled at its workers down the years. One of the bargaining strategies commonly used by all firms is to argue that unless labour costs are lowered immediately the prospects for future investment are bleak. A firm certainly need not be a transnational to do this. But when it is, it has the added ability to credibly threaten workers in any one country that failure to accept lower labour costs now will mean future investment elsewhere in the transnational's global empire. This can be credible precisely because it does have a global empire. This contrasts to a firm producing in one country and facing a united workforce; there is then no 'elsewhere' to throw in their faces (at least not in such a credible sense).

Ford's use of this strategy is clearly felt by Friedman (1977) to be an important feature of its industrial relations.[30] More specifically this is shown in Steuer and Gennard's (1972) report that in February 1970 Henry Ford was questioned by Hailwood shop stewards. They were concerned about rumours of new investment going to Germany rather than the UK, it being known that Detroit was unhappy with UK industrial relations. This story is taken up by ILO (1976). In 1971 there was a strike at Ford in Britain.

While this dispute was underway ... Henry Ford ... was reported to have declared that parts of the Ford Escort and Cortina models ... would in future no longer be made in the United Kingdom but would be manufactured in Asia ... Mr Ford came to London shortly thereafter, and in a meeting with (then) British Prime Minister Heath, he is reported to have let it be known, with regard to the company's labour difficulties, that if improvements were not forthcoming, the company would take its business elsewhere. (p.21–2)

Furthermore the threats are seemingly not empty:

In 1973 when the company decided to locate the bulk of its small car engine production in the United States (for the Pinto model, sold largely in the United States), the *Financial Times* (22 June) reported: 'It is no secret that industrial disputes in Britain priced the United Kingdom out of the market ...' The same paper added, 'There was, of course, no guarantee that Britain would ever have been selected for such a major development but the comments of Henry Ford ... (in) the early part of the year made it clear that the United Kingdom had dropped out of the running ...' The same report added, 'the fear of similar labour unrest in Germany in the future may have entered into the company' decision to locate the plant in the United States. (p.22)

Meanwhile, coming more up to date, it is clear from *Financial Times* reports that the threats at Ford are continuing. Ford's employee relations director, Paul Roots, is said to have told the UK unions in 1983 that labour costs were too high:

'This year, to date, we have achieved only 62 to 64 per cent of capacity at Halewood and Dagenham against 100 per cent at Saarlouis in West Germany and 96 per cent at Valencia, Spain,' he said. 'If we do not get our costs down we cannot compete and if we cannot compete we will not survive in Britain as a manufacturing company.'[31]

And the following year Ford of Europe's Vice-President for

Manufacturing, Mr Hayden, delivered the same message to workers in dispute with the company over investment plans:

> Although Mr Hayden denied that Ford was running down its British plants, he gave a stiff warning that the consequences for future investment would be serious if the productivity gap with European plants was not closed.[32]

Clearly little has changed down the years.

This leaves us with a catalogue of instances that can permit little doubt that divide and rule is important to understanding the activities of one of the largest companies in the world. The difficulty with this sort of evidence is that it is uncertain just how typical Ford is. But to say the least, it seems extremely unlikely that it is very unusual. Rather we can reasonably expect Ford to be typical. So this is also clear evidence that divide and rule is an important reason for the existence of transnationals. Again it goes to the heart of the matter and again it points to a clear conclusion. If Ford sees divide and rule as an opportunity for increased profits, so also will others. Indeed, the very fact that Ford can be seen to use the strategy means others will do likewise, on the basis that if it can yield profits for Ford it can yield profits for them – what is good enough for Ford will be good enough for other firms.[33] Not that good for Ford means good all round. Increased profits, yes. But also the possibility of worsening working conditions, for example, of a lower share of income going to wages, and of unemployment. Somebody, somewhere will be made to pay for the rise in profits.

NOTES

1. The exact nature of the conflict is not always simple. For example it has been argued that workers derive utility from increasing effort (see Marginson's (1986) survey) and clearly in so far as it goes employers will be happy to go along with this. But for us the important point is that there is conflict.
2. See the evidence of collusion over wages in Forsyth's (1972) survey of Scottish firms. The existence of localised labour markets is also likely to be important here because this will limit the number of firms colluding in any one situation.

3. It is not simply collective bargaining that is in issue. For instance, contacts by workers to foster information sharing are important, see for example Enderwick (1985).
4. See also Preiser (1971).
5. See also Lane's (1982) discussion of the difficulties faced by British trade unionists in multi-plant firms operating solely in the UK.
6. This hypothesis sees firms dividing their workers when they actually produce in various countries. A counterpart is where firms contemplating new investment divide potential employees. That is, for example, if firm A is to establish new production facilities it will bargain with potential employees for the lowest labour costs; if it bargains with divided potential employees – e.g. with workers in the Philippines and workers in the UK – it will tend to secure lower costs.
7. In his 'eclectic' theory Dunning (1980) suggests that transnationals may be able 'to reduce the impact of strikes or industrial unrest in one country by operating parallel production capacity in another . . .' (p.10). Nevertheless, Dunning's theory is very different from our approach, as Chapter 2 indicated.
8. The comparison being made here is a firm manufacturing shirts by cutting and sewing cloth in the UK versus a firm doing the same thing but in the UK and the Philippines. This is not to deny that different comparisons could be made. For example, between the bargaining power of labour when it is employed by a firm whose sole activity is to cut cloth in the UK and when it is employed by a firm which cuts cloth in the UK and sews this into shirts in the Philippines. Then UK labour may have more bargaining power when it is part of the wider operation encompassing the Philippines, other things being equal. (Simply because a strike in the UK would cause disruption in the Philippines by stopping work there once any stocks of cut cloth were exhausted.) But introducing these other comparisons does not undermine our divide-and-rule analysis; its very point is to take the activities of a particular firm and compare labour costs when *those* activities are carried out in one versus more than one country.
9. There is a vast literature on this. For a starting point, see for example the survey in Jessop (1977).
10. (i) A powerful bargaining counter for firms is the threat to produce elsewhere; for governments sensitive about unemployment in a world plagued by stagnation, this will carry considerable weight. (ii) Transnationals bargaining with nation states is dramatically illustrated by a story in the *Financial Times* on 27 August 1986. This tells of 25 transnational companies issuing a public ultimatum to the Pakistan government that unless they are allowed substantial rises in retail prices they will cut retailers margins to encourage retailers to go on strike.
11. See Chandler (1962) and Williamson (1970).
12. This is not to say why transnationals arise; it merely refers to the ability to produce in more than one country. It illustrates how firms can separate their workers into different groups yet maintain what Marglin (1974) calls the all-important 'supervision and discipline' of those workers – i.e. maintain control of the work process.

13. See again Chapter 2, especially the discussion of Benetton.
14. The endogeneity of such factors is of paramount importance.
15. Note also the clear rejection of the Coasian focus on market versus non-market exchanges.
16. Unlike the Hymer/Kindelberger approach, our analysis does not rely on the existence of such costs, as was pointed out in the footnotes of Chapter 2.
17. See also Marglin (1984).
18. See again Chapter 2 for a discussion of this point.
19. Hymer looks at the global distribution of three levels of decision-making and argues that top management will be located in the world's major cities. This is slightly different to our focus on strategic decision-makers as in the eyes of many these are not managers, see for instance Pitelis and Sugden (1986). Nevertheless Hymer (1972) is in general perfectly consistent with our analysis.
20. See Steuer and Gennard (1971), Gennard (1972), Dunning (1976), ILO (1976a) – giving a useful general survey – and Dunning and Morgan (1980).
21. Steuer and Gennard (1971), referring to the UK, note: 'the foreign subsidiary, particularly the American-owned firm, is alleged to utilise labour more effectively, which could be a nice way of saying people work harder' (p.119).
22. Our earlier analysis explaining why wage rates could be higher in transnationals would also explain why labour costs could be higher. Thus it would explain, for instance, what ILO (1976a) refers to as the widely accepted proposition that in underdeveloped countries conditions of work are often superior for employees of transnationals.
23. Strictly speaking the use of internationally spread facilities to counter union power does not mean that this is why the facilities were spread in the first place. But it is certainly a strong indication.
24. Comments from a Conference Report.
25. Statement from a Congress.
26. Daniel Benedict, 'Multinational Companies: Their Relations with the Workers', report to a Conference on Industrial Relations in the European Community of the Royal Institute of International Affairs, London, 1973.
27. They survey 50 in all, 13 having experience with non-US-owned companies.
28. They surveyed 29 companies in all.
29. This also shows how Ford uses more than one assembly point, a fact picked out by Friedman (1977) in his discussion of multisourcing in the car industry.
30. 'One of the most significant features of industrial relations in the UK motor industry from the mid-1960s has been the ever-present threat, particularly coming from Chrysler and Ford, to shift operations to other countries' (Friedman (1977), p.238).
31. 29 October 1983. Friedman (1977) refers to Ford using the pace of

production in its Continental plants as 'a yardstick and a driving stick' for UK workers.
32. 23 February, 1984.
33. A further, more specific, aspect to this is matching behaviour by rivals along the lines of our discussion in Chapter 2.

5 Transnational Corporations and Stagnation

Earlier chapters have focused on the growth in power of the transnationals and the implications of this for the workings of product and labour markets. Throughout, the consequences for various dimensions of the distribution of income were identified. This chapter will extend the analysis by focusing on the impact of such redistributions of income on the evolution of the macroeconomy. It has frequently been argued that the development of the monopoly capitalist system will, sooner or later, lead to a stagnationist tendency rather than a long-run, full-employment equilibrium. We shall present the basic argument before going on to examine more directly the implications for this process of the transnational control of production and markets by the dominant firms within the system. Is the issue of stagnation likely to be more or less pressing in a world dominated by such transnational organisations? Our analysis points fairly unambiguously to the conclusion that stagnation will be a more pressing issue in such a world, not only because it will become more likely, but that it will also become more unmanageable without quite radical changes in the way the international economy is regulated.

MONOPOLISATION AND STAGNATION

We established in Chapter 3 significant links between the evolving transnational control of production and general

monopolisation tendencies. The argument advanced in monopoly capitalism theory is that such monopolising tendencies
within the older industrialised countries of the world would
lead eventually to a stagnation tendency due to a deficiency of
aggregate demand within that part of the world economic
system and this in turn would lead to a more general stagnation.[1] Taking Cowling (1982) as illustrative of this view, we
inevitably adopt a European post-World War II perspective
on these linkages between the evolving industrial structure of
an economy and its macroeconomic characteristics. The
analysis starts with the prediction and observation of substantial increases in concentration in most markets, enhanced and
sustained by rising transnationalism, which are expected to
result in the increase in prices relative to marginal costs, and
therefore to an increase in the share of profits plus overhead
costs in value-added – it is argued that neither worker pressure
nor import-penetration will reverse this tendency (see
Chapters 3 and 4). The *potential* therefore clearly exists for an
increase in the share of profits, but whether or not this is
realised depends on the impact of the process on aggregate
demand. The immediate impact would be a downward re-
vision in planned investment in line with the planned reduction in the rate of output (or its growth rate) within those
sectors where the degree of monopoly has increased. The
reduction in aggregate investment, in the absence of compensating adjustments elsewhere, would lead to a reduction in
the level of profits in the total system, which would lead to
further cutbacks in investment and thus generate a cumulative
process of decline.[2] Compensating, upward adjustments in
investment elsewhere may of course take place as a result of
the underlying tendency for the potential share of profits to
increase – for example, via a process of diversification. However such adjustments are likely to involve quite considerable
lags, due to the uncertainty surrounding profit expectations
and the long gestation periods involved in new investment
projects, coupled with the fact that the planned cutbacks in
those sectors experiencing an increase in the degree of monopoly become unplanned cutbacks elsewhere in the system.
Empirical observation appears unambiguous – the negative
impact on investment of the increase in surplus capacity

appears to dominate. For example, Burman (1970) concluded, on the basis of a fairly comprehensive survey of empirical results, that 'most of the variation in manufacturing investment is due to variations in capacity utilisation', and later results, for example by Panic and Vernon (1975) and Peretz (1976), have given strong support to such an interpretation.

Clearly, any deficiency in investment could be made up by an increase in consumption out of the increased potential flow of profits arising from the monopolisation tendency, so that aggregate demand could be maintained. However, this is unlikely to happen fast enough nor to the required extent, given that profit recipients receive their income less frequently than wage-earners and also tend to have much lower propensities to consume (see, for example, Pitelis, 1982). There is also the question of whether such households will have access to the increased flow of profits. For a variety of reasons corporations prefer to retain profits rather than distribute them and it has been observed that the level of aggregate retentions has a substantial positive impact on the level of aggregate savings (see, for example, Pitelis, 1984). However, managerialism, reflected in rising intra-corporation consumption out of non-reported profits, and here we refer to all those expenditures *within* the corporation which contribute directly to managerial utility but which represents a deduction from profits, many, or perhaps most, of the trappings of office, could provide at least a partial antidote to such a deficiency in demand, but it contains its own contradictions. Although in aggregate, by tending to maintain demand, managerialism serves to maintain profits, it will be seen as something to be minimised by those (shareholders) interested in the flow of reported profits. Thus, although the growth of giant firms operating in oligopolistic markets gives rise to a substantial growth in managerial discretion arising as a result of their increasing isolation from the sanctions of both capital and product markets, with all the associated expenditures which that is likely to entail, such discretion will inevitably lead to measures to curtail it. The innovation of efficient *internal* control systems, like the multi-divisional organisational form which decentralises operational responsibility to production divisions whilst centralising control of capital flows, thus creating an efficient and well-informed internal capital market, will impose very real limits on the ability of managerial capitalism to overcome a latent tendency to stagnation.

In principle other adjustments are possible. Aggregate demand could be maintained via a growing net export surplus, but there is little reason to suggest that this is likely to follow a rise in the degree of monopoly within any particular economy; indeed just the reverse could happen – as prices rise, imports could be drawn in by such a change. If the rise in the degree of monopoly is a general trend within the world industrial system as a whole, then it is even less likely that a growing export surplus could be maintained over an extended period, since it would raise the issue of how the rest of the world's growing trade deficit was to be financed. The present international debt crisis could be seen as a consequence of a rising degree of monopoly in the industrial and energy sectors of the world economy, and the imposed, deflationary response will further deepen the world slump.

Of course, if all else fails, governments could step in to manage aggregate demand in order to secure the full employment of resources. Thus the negative impact of a rising degree of monopoly on aggregate demand could be fully offset by a rising budget deficit. But clearly we cannot necessarily assume this sort of response. Maintaining full employment inevitably changes the balance of power between capital and labour, with a variety of consequences, and the state will not usually be a disinterested observer of this process. We have seen, over our recent history, how monetarism has replaced Keynesianism, not only in Thatcher's Britain, but also earlier in Callaghan's Britain and more generally within the national governments and supra-national institutions of the world's advanced industrial countries. As long ago as 1979 the International Monetary Fund, the World Bank, OECD and GATT were united in demanding an end to Keynesian policies. For them demand management was dead.[3] The apparently Keynesian policies of the present US administration seem to have arisen largely fortuitously out of the supply-side economics and military expansion of the Reagan administration.

Thus, given the unwillingness of governments to intervene at certain conjunctures, stagnation arising from a monopolisation tendency remains a distinct possibility: not an inevitable outcome at any particular period of history but nevertheless an inevitable consequence at some stage in the unravelling of the monopoly capitalist system. However, some have argued the existence of a way out. Aggregate demand could be maintained by reducing the aggregate propensity to save via advertising and product innovation, and we can rely on the system of monopoly capitalism to generate just such a response. Whilst this sort of investment has some attractive properties in that it stimulates demand without at the same time directly raising the productive capacity of the system, and therefore reposing the initial question of the full utilisation of capacity, as does investment in plant and equipment (see Rothschild, 1982), it would seem incapable of properly fulfilling this role given its essentially procyclical character. Whilst we are concerned with a long-term tendency this is not separable from the process of cyclical fluctuation – the long-term tendency is embedded in the short-term cycle and cannot be isolated from it. Advertising and product innovation tend to mimic the behaviour of investment in general and so seem ill-equipped to fill the role of replacing investment within the structure of aggregate demand.

It may therefore be concluded that, although mechanisms are available to mitigate any stagnationist tendency precipitated by a tendency for the degree of monopoly to increase, partly as a result of rising transnationalism, none is automatic. It has also been observed that each contains its own contradictions. For example, although raising the level of investment may mitigate the short-term problem of an insufficient level of effective demand arising from an underlying redistribution of income from those with a high propensity to consume to those with a much lower one, nevertheless the underlying issue will become more pressing as the extra capacity provided by the increased investment comes on stream. Similarly with advertising. Whilst serving to raise demand for the output of the system it also serves to create conditions in product markets conducive to a higher observed degree of monopoly and thus to a redistribution of income which tends to reduce the effective demand for the output of the system. It would appear to remain the case that a stagnationist tendency is an inevitable consequence of the maturing of the monopoly capitalist system.[4]

THE SOCIALISATION OF CAPITAL AND STAGNATION

An alternative, and complementary, view of the link between the evolution of the capitalist system and the emergence of a stagnationist tendency has recently been put forward by Christos Pitelis (1985). He argues that the process of capital accumulation inevitably leads to the increased socialisation of capital. Initially this is achieved via the growth in discretionary shareholdings but at a later stage compulsory shareholding associated with the 'pension funds revolution' takes the leading role. The growth of pension funds, coupled with the growth in corporate retained earnings, appears to have had a major impact in raising the ratio of aggregate savings to private disposable income. The net inflow in life assurance and pension funds has increased as a ratio to private disposable income from 3.59 per cent in the decade 1954/63 to 4.44 per cent in 1964/73, and to 5.94 per cent in 1974/83, and corporate retained earnings increased in similar fashion from 12.41 per cent, to 13.08 per cent and finally to 15.75 per cent. The question may then be raised, did this simply substitute for a decline in personal savings? In fact personal savings increased over the same period from 1.44 per cent, to 3.77 per cent, and finally to 5 per cent. Econometric work has confirmed that personal savings add on to corporate savings rather than substituting for them. Thus Pitelis has unearthed an alternative source of a stagnationist tendency within an evolving advanced capitalist system – a declining propensity to consume related to the increasing socialisation of capital. In the case of both the monopolisation of product markets and socialisation of capital origins of stagnation there is a clear demand-side rationale for looking abroad, either in terms of markets for the output of surplus capacity or in terms of investment opportunities. In either case we may detect the origins, or the further development, of the transnational organisation of production being related to demand side developments within the advanced industrial countries.

Meanwhile in the next section we offer a supply-side explanation of the origin of stagnationist tendencies within specific countries: a supply-side explanation which is based on the activities of the transnationals.

TRANSNATIONAL PRODUCTION AND DEINDUSTRIALISATION

We have offered two, complementary, demand-side explanations of stagnation, in both of which transnationalism has a role, which will be explored in detail at a later stage. We now seek to make clear that the emergence of such a stagnationist tendency within a specific country at a particular point in history may have a supply-side explanation. Associated with the evolution of the monopoly capitalist system, with its growth of ever more dominant giant firms, is the related increase in the power and militancy of organised labour. This in turn is likely to lead to an accelerating wage-price spiral coupled with political developments which culminate in the growth of the social wage; that is state expenditures biased in favour of workers and their families. Capital flight to other locations more conducive to capital accumulation will tend to follow wherever conditions facilitate it. The present era, where production and markets are controlled by giant corporations with a transnational base and where national and international controls over trade and capital flows have been progressively reduced, with certain exceptions like the continuing tension over Japan, provide those conditions. The combination of unified international markets and giant international firms bestriding them provides a ready mechanism for the processes of deindustrialisation to develop wherever the conditions for capitalist accumulation are weakened. In contrast to the earlier history of the development of monopolies and cartels around the turn of the twentieth century, when protectionism was demanded to restrict or eliminate foreign competition in both domestic and colonial markets, the present period is characterised by demands on the part of the giant, transnational corporations for free trade and the supranational institutions to pursue and sanction it:[5] a global freedom to pursue accumulation, given their own dominance within the global system and given the threat, or potential threat of organised labour and universal suffrage at the level of the nation-state. It might be said we now have a neo-imperialism of free trade in similar vein to the nineteenth-century British imperialism of free trade,[6] but this time, rather than being of national origin – rather than reflecting national rivalry – the imperialism is that of the transnationals. We now need to enquire into the new international division of labour that these forces have created or will create.[7] We are therefore continuing the theme developed in Chapter 4.

The old international division of labour divided the world up into the advanced industrial countries and the backward primary producers, with international trade between these groups of countries dominating world trade. International firms, if they existed in production, were involved in extracting primary products from the backward countries. With the evolution of the transnational corporation this simple dichotomy was progressively destroyed. Initially the switching of production and investment took place between centre and periphery within the industrialised countries or to their geographical neighbours. Thus US corporations invested in Europe and Mexico, Western European-based corporations invested in their southern neighbours and Ireland and, more recently, Japanese corporations invested in South Korea and Taiwan. Whilst such moves could be stimulated by a myriad of causes it seems clear that an all-pervading, general influence would be the existence of, and changes in, unit labour cost differentials reflecting differences in the relative power and militancy of labour. By extension, an increasing tendency to switch production and investment away from the advanced industrial countries to the unindustrialised or newly industrialising countries would be expected.[8] This tendency would occur because of rising worker power and militancy *generally* in the older industrial countries, associated with the long boom of the quarter-century post-World War II, implying rising relative wages and falling relative productivity, and because of the growth of a deskilling technology. The actual timing of such shifts would depend on the innovation and diffusion of corporate structures capable of handling such global production patterns and of systems of communication

and transportation which would facilitate it. The rapid diffusion of the multi-divisional organisational structure across the
giant corporations of the capitalist world, partly inspired by
the objective of going national within the United States or
transnational in the case of corporations based in other
countries, has provided an ideal environment for the flexible
switching of capital flows within the global economy. Rather
than simply delaying capitalism's early bureaucratic demise
the advent of this organisational innovation has directly
contributed to the conversion of the major corporations to
their present global status and reach. The decentralisation of
responsibility for operational decision-making coupled with
the efficient centralised control of capital flows allows the
modern corporation flexibility to adapt to an increasing
number of satellite production units around the globe whilst
retaining strategic control from headquarters in some distant
key city. The more recent revolution in information technology has already played a significant role in the same
process and will clearly continue as a major accommodating
factor.

Given the existence of such flexible corporate structures, the
decomposition of complex processes so that only unskilled
labour is needed in production, and an information technology which renders geographical distance unimportant, the
social and economic infrastructure of the advanced industrial
countries remains the only significant economic impediment
on the supply side to a wholesale transfer of industrial
production to the low-wage countries, so long as transportation costs do not erode the labour cost advantages. It is also
important to recall from our earlier discussion of the nature of
the firm (Chapter 2), that the switching of production between
the older industrialised centres and the newly emerging industrial periphery is not entirely dependent on the growth of the
transnational *ownership* of production facilities: it can also
reflect the growth of a new putting-out system, which may
have a purely domestic basis, but which will often have an
international one. Thus an increasingly popular device for
circumventing a powerful and well-organised labour force,
which evolved within the conducive atmosphere of the large
plant in the older industrial areas over the Long Boom, has

been the vertical disintegration of production, but within the control of the giant firm (see Chapters 2 and 4). More and more of the work is subcontracted out; to a domestic, relatively competitive structure of suppliers, or to foreign suppliers, where the producers face a less powerful and less well-organised labour force. Partly this may represent a first step in a process of transition where production as a whole is shifted from a regime or a country with a well-organised labour force to alternative locations, domestic or foreign, where this is not the case.[9] As we have maintained earlier, whatever the final form, the issue of control, within the process of production and within markets, is more fundamental than the ownership of the production units themselves. The current general promotion of small business in most advanced industrial countries is explicable in these terms. Rather than being a threat to the giant corporation it fits in perfectly with their strategy of moving production away from those centres where they have tended to lose control, and will in turn serve to circumscribe the power of organised labour in those production units which must of necessity, at least in the short-term, remain in the old-established centres.

Increasingly the major corporations will become coordinating agencies for large numbers of production units, each supplying services to the dominant organisation at competitive rates and paying competitive wages.[10] This represents an extension of the notion of the multi-divisional corporation with its centralisation of strategic, capital allocation decisions, coupled with the decentralisation of operational production decisions. Now strategic marketing and production decisions are being added to the headquarters function, with small business in satellite relation with the dominant corporation, often tied in with long-term contracts. The dominant corporations' basic role is then to secure an allocation of production, internally *or externally*, consistent with cost-minimisation, whilst maintaining or enhancing market control. This system of control may include a retail sector in the same internal or external satellite relations with the dominant supplying corporation, or the retail sector itself may be the dominant element in the system of control. Thus the British Shoe Corporation is a dominant element in shoe retailing, has some production units of its own, but is also a major importer of shoes produced by other firms; whilst Marks and Spencer has long-term contracts with external suppliers, British and foreign; and the major clothes retailers dominate a system of small-scale producers via various types of putting-out arrangements, again within Britain and abroad. GEC, one of the British pioneers in the adoption of the multi-divisional structure and a dominant element in the British electrical industry, is moving towards dividing up its existing structure into autonomous companies, and continues to use its own trademarks and advertising to sell goods which are to a substantial degree foreign sourced – sometimes intra-corporate, and in other cases inter-firm, although in most cases incorporated within the new theoretical definition of the firm we have advanced in Chapter 2.

The central point is that although systems will differ, the aim of the giant corporation will be the control of a sector of the relevant economy so that the maximum level of profits can be squeezed from it. Whilst the ownership of production facilities by such giants may contribute to this objective, and has undoubtedly provided the initial platform for dominance, this is generally neither necessary nor sufficient. So long as the corporation retains its control of the market for the product, for example via long-term contracts coupled with its prior investment in advertising, product differentiation and the distribution network, independent producers could be allowed to make all operating/production decisions.[11] The generally observed tendency is towards subcontracting to other (usually smaller) capitalist organisations, or to individual households (examples can be observed in textiles and computer software), at home or abroad, thus circumventing some of the difficulties giant organisations will inevitably generate as a result of the growth in power of organised labour, or switching production and investment to new sites where labour is unorganised, has no history of large-scale organisation or has been cowed by a repressive regime. Such tendencies will be manifest *within* as well as *between* countries – between the 'Snowbelt' and the 'Sunbelt' within the United States,[12] as well as between the United States and Mexico or Brazil; between older and newer industrial areas within the

UK, as well as between the UK and Malaysia or Singapore. The central feature is an increasing geographical flexibility of capitalist production which allows capital to escape the clutches of organised labour and must ultimately weaken the position of such labour in the areas of production which remain.

Globalism of this sort could of course work the other way – rather than moving jobs to the (unorganised) workers, domestically or internationally, (unorganised) workers could be moved to the jobs. This was the dominant pattern of the long boom. The old division of labour persisted at the level of nation-states but the workforce, at least in the industrial countries, was internationalised. The internationalisation of production had a very specific meaning. The impediment to industrial expansion posed by relatively full employment in the advanced industrial countries was removed by substantial migrations from the periphery. But, as Adam (1975) shows, this process started to falter in the late 1960s to early 1970s, due to rising wage demands, with General Motors complaining about the 'unpredictability' of the American labour market, and leaders of West German corporations stressing the necessity and inevitably of international sourcing in response to the 'unjustified' wage demands of 1972/73. He also makes the interesting point that it is not sufficient to say that the recession-induced unemployment of that period led to the cutback in foreign workers because it was the growth in *external* investment which led to the jobs cutback in West Germany. One of the underlying reasons for the switch was undoubtedly the growing resistance to immigration which in turn strengthened the position of labour in such economies. The consequence has been a growth in managed trade and decline in managed migration.

At this point it would be useful to put Japanese expansionism into perspective since it is often argued that deindustrialisation within the US and Europe has been induced by the rising dominance of Japanese capital, and thus the relative decline in European and American capital – i.e. a new international division of labour may have come about, but it has not been managed or controlled by the giant corporations of the old order; rather a new order prevails. When analysing the relative performance of national economies this may appear to be so. Japan increased its share of world industrial production and exports throughout the 1960s and 1970s while the US and Europe (in aggregate) experienced declining shares. However if we measure changes in world sales classi-fied by the nationality of the parent company a very different picture emerges. Whilst Japanese industrial capital made considerable gains at the expense of particularly US capital in the 1960s, almost no further advance was achieved in the 1970s. The advance of European industrial capital since 1967 has considerably exceeded that of Japanese industrial capital and this must have been achieved by a relatively rapid expansion of foreign production. A significant part of this is undoubtedly due to the rising share of oil industry revenue, but this serves as a reminder of the dominance of European (and American) capital in the markets for many strategic raw materials.[13] Our conclusion must be that the deindustrialisa-tion the West as a whole has experienced in the 1970s and early 1980s cannot be ascribed to Japanese expansionism. The high relative growth rate of Japanese industrial capital in the 1960s took place in a period of relative buoyancy in economic activity in the West. It seems clear that the forces of deindus-trialisation which have been most obvious in Europe, have been most active during a period when European industrial capital was increasing its share of the world economy. This is entirely in line with the argument made in this chapter.

DEINDUSTRIALISATION: THE CASE OF BRITAIN

Whilst there was an observed tendency for the capitalist system as a whole to enter an apparent long-term downswing in the 1970s, the experience of the British economy has been an extreme one and may be at least partly related to the relatively high degree of internationalisation of British capital, both industrial and financial. The United Kingdom stands out as second only to the United States in terms of overseas direct investment in the world economy during the period 1967–78 (see UNCTNC, 1983). In 1967 the United Kingdom accounted for 15.6 per cent of the total of foreign direct investment from developed market economies, in contrast to West Germany's share of 2.6 per cent and Japan's 1.3 per cent. Whilst by 1978 the share of the United Kingdom had dropped to 11 per cent it still remained substantially in excess of West Germany (8.5 per cent) and Japan (7.2 per cent). It is also notable that foreign direct investment is much more important for the United Kingdom than for the United States. The strong international links and commitments imply that money capital can be readily shifted abroad and, in consequence, the rate of investment within the domestic economy may be retarded. This will be most obviously the case where investment abroad is used to replace the domestic sourcing of the British market by foreign sourcing, or where exports from Britain are being replaced by overseas production, but it can also apply generally as the financing of British investment tends to dry up. Whilst the giants will always be able to get the financing they require, newer and smaller firms will often face difficulties, and their position in the British economy, in contrast to the other European economies and the United States, will be that much more vulnerable.[14] This may help to explain why the British economy has a much weaker small firm sector than, for example, West Germany and the United States, and correspondingly why the giant corporations in Britain tend to be much more dominant. The argument that giantism is required for dynamism and international competitiveness hardly seems to hold water when we note that the most undynamic and uncompetitive economy also possesses most of the giant firms in Europe.[15]

The short-run impact of the retarding of domestic investment, if uncompensated by other forms of expenditure, is a cutback in output and employment in Britain. The longer-term impact is that domestic productivity growth falls relative to other economies without such international connections, which in turn leads to lower levels of investment in new processes and products and therefore to a relative decline in internal and external demand for the output of the British economy. This leads into a process of cumulative causation. A relative decline in external demand feeds through, via a variety of mechanisms, into a relative decline in the growth of output, productivity, innovation and capital stock, which in turn leads to a further twist in the relative decline in the growth of external demand for British output. The British economy has entered the vicious circle of relative decline partly because of the special international connections of British capital, whereas in contrast the European economies and Japan, largely, and until very recently, exploiting foreign markets from a *domestic* production base, have, as a result, entered the virtuous circle of cumulative causation, with productivity growth responding to the growth in output following external demand. Success breeds success, failure breeds failure, *at the level of the national economy*, but, as we have already seen, we should distinguish carefully between the success of national *economies* and the success of national *capitals*. However, in the British case, it could be argued that the relative demise of the national economy has gone so far as to have had a marked deleterious effect on the national capital. Despite its strong and pervasive international connections, British capital's lack of a strong domestic base has probably severely damaged its future prospects. One question which might be raised about this story is why the British state has not intervened to secure an escape from the vicious circle of relative decline. Limited attempts have been made from time to time but they have foundered on their implicit unwillingness to address the root cause. As a result, brief periods of expansion have been followed inevitably by sharp cutbacks – the stop–go history of the 1950s and 1960s, which finally led in the mid-1970s to a move away from Keynesian to monetarist policies as the rate of inflation increased. Given the lack of success of the British economy there was a boiling-up of worker dissatisfaction which was translated into inflationary pressure. Thus the forces which led to the lack of success, like the international posture of British capital, inevitably led to the adoption of deflationary policies by the state, which in turn led, via an extended process of cumulative causation, to further deterioration in the relative performance of the British economy and at the same time weakened the position of British capital in its global stance.

What of the empirical evidence on the role of the transnationals in the deindustrialisation of the British economy? Stopford and Turner (1985) report that for their sample of 58

UK transnationals over the period 1972–83, the total domestic job loss was 600,000, whereas jobs overseas went up by 200,000. Gaffikin and Nickson (1984) concluded that for ten West Midlands-based transnationals, domestic employment fell by 31 per cent over the period 1978–82 whilst overseas employment increased by 2 per cent over this period of relative depression. Both observations are consistent with the argument made above, but Stopford and Turner go on to suggest that the proportionate decline in domestic employment they observe for their UK transnationals is the same as that for UK domestic firms, whilst in the case of foreign-controlled transnationals employment in the United Kingdom actually rose. However, it is clear from the qualifications they make that the company data they use are simply not appropriate for the task in hand. The typically giant transnational firms which enter their sample tend to dominate merger and takeover activity within the United Kingdom. Thus we might expect that these firms will tend to grow substantially over time through such acquisitions. Thus comparisons between transnationals and purely domestic firms will be biased by the differential acquisition effect.[16] In addition it would be necessary to calculate the knock-on effect on purely domestic firms of the cutbacks in domestic production and investment by the dominant transnationals. In the case of firms producing solely to service the transnationals the resulting employment cutbacks are likely to be *more* than proportional since the strategic core of the transnational is maintained as a managerial and technical hierarchy supervising and servicing a global empire, whereas the same would not be true of the smaller, domestic supplier. Until someone attempts a more rigorous analysis, we have very little to go on, although the necessary corrections would indicate that domestic employment loss from the British transnationals has been greater than from domestic firms given that the uncorrected figures indicate equal proportional loss. However, we can readily accept that the transnationals are not the only culprits. Some of the biggest job losses in recent years have come from the dismantling of major manufacturing firms in the public sector – British Steel and British Leyland – as part of the government's attempts to reduce its losses in these sectors.

A NEGATIVE-SUM GLOBAL GAME

In the previous two sections we have attempted to demonstrate how the processes of deindustrialisation can be related to the activities of the transnationals over the recent history of the advanced industrial countries. Although the timing and impact will vary, we have suggested a certain inevitability to such developments so long as the transnationals are largely unimpeded in their locational decisions. Whilst for much of their history success may breed success for the advanced industrial countries, eventually the growth in unit labour costs arising from increasing union power and militancy resulting from the concentration and centralisation of capital in these economies, will prompt decisions to move production to countries where lower unit labour costs prevail. Innovations to enable such moves will be stimulated by the existence of such increasing cost differentials. As we have argued earlier, such developments do not imply the decline of the major corporations based in the advanced industrial countries, simply a reallocation of their production and employment patterns. We need now to assess the global consequences for production and employment of such a global game. Whilst deindustrialisation may be the consequence for the older industrialised cities, regions and countries, will this be simply offset by the creation of industrialisation elsewhere?

It is often argued that deindustrialisation and industrialisation are simply mirror-images of each other. Industrial growth and decline are simply offsetting tendencies within the global system, representing part of a zero-sum, or even positive-sum, global game. Those who believe in a self-regulating market mechanism would see the transnational corporation as a suitably efficient and flexible capital-allocating device capable of securing an efficient allocation of resources at a global level. The shift of simple production processes from the advanced industrial countries to the developing countries would, at one and the same time, release an educated and skilled labour force for more sophisticated forms of production, whilst allowing labour in the Third World to move from relatively unproductive employment in the agricultural sector to more highly productive employment in industry. Full employment, according to this view, is the norm and would be maintained as the world economic system adapted smoothly to new opportunities. Some transitional or frictional unemployment may be observed, but this would be of little significance compared with the enormous rewards attached to such a global reallocation of production.

Given the present global economic crisis, this view will appear unrealistic to at least a segment of the prevailing orthodoxy and they will argue that the position can be restored by an international Keynesian intervention to secure a global demand expansion which will allow the mechanism described above to operate without the frictions which have arisen as a result of the global dislocations following the OPEC crisis of the early 1970s. Thus a basically efficient process for the allocation of the world's material resources could be provided with a suitable international macroeconomic environment in which to operate. Whilst ignoring the problem of explaining how such a system could have degenerated into its present crisis, such a policy of global reflation would be advocated on what are claimed to be pragmatic, non-ideological grounds. The *Brandt Report* captures the flavour of this position.

In contrast to these alternative versions of the prevailing orthodoxy, we wish to argue that the process of global industrialisation and deindustrialisation, which is being currently orchestrated by the transnationals, is a socially inefficient and undemocratic process. Capital has become increasingly mobile, leaving a trail of social disruption in its wake and imposing huge growth costs on the industrialising nations. Whilst it will be privately efficient for each transnational corporation to adopt such an existence, reflecting as it does an appropriate response to rising labour costs, the opportunities offered by improvement in communications and transportation and by a more flexible production technology and internal organisational structure, it means that an international transmission mechanism for production, investment and jobs will have been largely adopted for income distributional reasons. Whenever workers act to raise wages, or control the intensity and duration of work, they will lose their jobs to other groups of less well-organised and less militant workers in other countries. Thus deindustrialisation is a consequence of the struggle between labour and capital in such a world. We can expect to see long swings of development and decline being inversely related across economies with different histories. The alternating long swings of international monopoly capital will follow the rise and fall of the power and militancy of labour.

The process is basically inefficient because it is motivated by issues of control and distribution – the control of the work process by those who hire labour, and distribution in favour of those who control the location of production, big capital and its representatives within the strategic core of the managerial hierarchy. Thus the allocation of production and investment is not guided primarily by questions of efficiency – that is, getting more output from given resources – but by the question of profitability, where profitability is determined by the price of labour and the amount of work that can be extracted at that price, assuming other costs are fixed. The process of deindustrialisation can therefore be initiated by increases in wages or reductions in the input of effort in one country (for example, as a result of workers establishing some degree of control over the pace of work) and may result in the industrialisation of a country where the output resulting from any *given* amount of effort is lower. Two points arise from this: first, the *direction* of movement is not determined by questions of social efficiency; and second, the *frequency* of movement will generally exceed the social optimum. Misdirection is possible because of distributional considerations – excessive frequency will occur because the transnationals are not faced with the full social costs of their locational decisions. Shifting production from country to country will not only mean that whole communities which have been built up to serve the interests of capital will simply be deserted, with all the social costs being absorbed by that society, but also the costs of social and economic infrastructure by the newly industrialising country will in turn be borne by that society. A socially efficient system would require these externalities be borne by the agent precipitating such relocation. If this were the case, such relocations would be much less frequent.

 · Thus the direction and frequency of locational change will tend to be socially inefficient in a world dominated by unregulated giant firms with a global reach. But the argument can be deepened. Not only are such giant firms flexible in their pursuit of profit on a global basis; they are also powerful. They are generally powerful enough to influence the terms under which they choose to operate. Not only do they *react* to the level of wages and the pace of work, they also *act* to determine them. Thus the distributional consequences are much more general, affecting those who remain in work as well as those who lose their jobs (see Chapter 4). The credible threat of the shift of production and investment will serve to hold down wages and raise the level of effort. By making investment conditional on the level of wage costs, transnationals may also be able to gain the cooperation of the state in securing the appropriate environment in which wage costs will tend to be held down. By threatening to export investment, profits taxes can be held down and subsidies for investment can be raised. Such threats will stimulate competitive profits tax-cutting and competitive subsidisation of investment by national governments which must ultimately work in favour of a redistribution towards profits.

TRANSNATIONALS AND DEMAND-SIDE EXPLANATIONS OF STAGNATION

The increasingly nomadic nature of capital, and its distributional implications, are also likely to induce a general global tendency to stagnation. Partly this is to do with the tendency towards the monopolisation of product markets which is served by the growing dominance of giant global corporations and which leads to problems of maintaining a level of aggregate demand in the system as a whole sufficient to avoid a significant increase in unemployed resources, both capital and labour. We have argued earlier that in a world of monopoly capitalism we cannot assume instantaneous adjustment by capitalists to the expected increased flow of profits – neither would we necessarily expect appropriate adjustments in other forms of expenditure. Thus distributional changes in income arising from a monopolisation tendency will, at certain conjunctures, turn into a stagnationist tendency. The question we are then faced with is, how does the growth of transnationalism affect this process?

First, as extensively explored in Chapter 3, transnationalism is one of the *mechanisms* whereby the monopolisation tendency evolves, just as the earlier nationalisation tendency of capital led to the growth of monopoly at the national level. Transnationalisation has introduced an additional dimension of control over the market – it brings control by giant firms to the pattern and dimensions of trade and therefore undermines the possible impact of trade in restraining monopoly or oligopoly pricing behaviour within national markets as well as promoting collusion within such markets. In the process of establishing such control these giant firms may engage in various forms of economic warfare, the outcome of which in the transitional period may be a reduction in price, although even this outcome is less likely than advertising and product rivalry which will tend to enhance rather than undermine the degree of monopoly.

Second, transnationalism results in the greater imbalance of power between capital and labour and therefore tends to hold down wage costs which may have implications for the distribution of income.[17] As we have explained earlier, to have an impact on distribution in a world of monopoly capitalism, changes in wage costs will either have to change the degree of monopoly (the mark-up of price on marginal cost) or the ratio of expenditure on materials to expenditure on wages. Whilst not inevitable, under certain conditions already identified (see Chapter 4), a reduction in wage costs can imply a reduction in wage share. It is also the case that the share of *overhead* labour will tend to fall under more general conditions as salary rates are held down.[18] Such developments will tend to reinforce the direct effects of monopolisation on distribution.

Third, the evolution of transnational production orchestrated exclusively, at least for much of the formative period of the process, by the giant corporations of the advanced industrial countries, will almost inevitably lead to the extension of the forces of monopoly capitalism into countries and indeed continents, where it initially had a less than secure footing. One can recognise that the impact of plants intended to supply the markets of the advanced industrial countries may have only a limited effect, but it is unlikely that things will remain at that stage. Increased infiltration of the institutions, mechanisms and ideas of monopoly capitalism will inevitably transform the nature of the economies of the newly industrialising countries. At such a point the intrusion may be seen as a dynamic and progressive force, and yet the seeds of stagnation are carried through into new territory and will ultimately grow and tend to dominate the progressive forces in the same way as in the older established industrial countries. We can also expect to see the recently industrialised countries subjected to the same forces of deindustrialisation as already experienced by the older industrialised countries as and when their unit labour costs begin to diverge from those which might be achieved in less-developed countries. Singapore may be an early example of such developments.

Thus, in the long term, we can expect that, as a result of the evolution of dominant transnationals and their spread across the world economy, the general degree of monopoly in product markets will tend to rise, this rise will be spread across a greater fraction of the world economy, and as a result the underlying stagnationist tendency of monopoly capitalism will be enhanced.

Transnationalism also has a role in serving to sustain the tendency for the propensity to save to increase as the socialisation of capital proceeds – a tendency we have explored earlier as a complementary explanation of stagnation. Given that such an increasing propensity to save is likely eventually to raise the issue of the realisation of profits in a world of monopoly capitalism, it may be argued that the whole process is likely to falter as profitable investment opportunities tend to dry up. Although there will still be an incentive on the part of those who control the major corporations to amass financial capital via, for example, retentions and pension funds, nevertheless there is likely to be increasing resistance to such pressure given that the prospective returns are falling within a stagnating economy. But as Pitelis (1985) has argued, this predicament may be avoided by going transnational. Funds which might otherwise have been invested in the domestic economy, or not saved, will now be able to flow smoothly to foreign locations, whilst still serving the direct interests of those controlling the corporations involved. Thus the initial aim of garnering the savings of a broader spectrum of the population in order to allow corporate empires to grow can be sustained by extending the firm internationally as opportunities to invest domestically contract as a direct result of the effect of the whole process on domestic aggregate demand. Transnational flexibility serves to maintain a second stagnationist tendency.

The impact of the two general tendencies to stagnation identified above will be accentuated by the associated political developments arising in a world where the power of the transnationals is growing. By acting generally to curtail the power of labour and the nation-state, the transnationals are acting to contain forces which may otherwise tend to redistribute income away from profits. While we might expect the advent of universal suffrage to lead to demands for the redistribution of income, wealth and power in favour of the majority, the existence of giant transnational centres of economic power will undermine such democratic demands. Similarly the efforts of organised labour to secure increases in the 'social wage' and legislation of benefit to itself will be similarly undermined. The consequence is that whereas a stagnationist tendency could be averted by appropriate redistributions via the political process, this will be rendered increasingly unlikely as a result of the increased political power provided by the transnational organisation of production.

But the political process is also affected in another way. The existence of transnational corporations serves to reduce the effectiveness of the policies of the nation-state aimed at securing full employment. Keynesian demand management policies will prove less effective because of the greater leakage via imports, for any one country, induced by the transnational organisation of production. Thus the incentive to adopt Keynesian policies will be weakened, whilst at the same time pressures to impose classical supply-side responses would increase. Deindustrialisation would appear to require that real wages be reduced, and yet this in itself would contribute to the stagnationist tendency induced by the redistributional tendencies already discussed. The system effect would be that the stagnationist tendency of the world economy would be augmented by general pressures to move away from Keynesian demand management and substitute policies requiring general wage-cutting. What may appear rational for one country, collectively will be irrational.[19]

FURTHER ACCENTUATING THE TENDENCY TOWARDS STAGNATION

We now turn to those characteristics of the system of transnational production which feed in *directly* to the processes of global stagnation rather than *indirectly* via either the redistribution of income, the socialisation of capital or the political process. They all turn on the limitations of the international planning of the allocation of production within one sector of the world economy. First, the additional flexibility offered by transnational production implies greater instability due to more frequent relocation and therefore income and expenditure loss in a world with considerable frictions. For countries (and regions) where production and investment is moving out, unemployment will inevitably rise and purchasing power will be lost. This will lead to a downward spiral in economic activity in general. The new nomadism will contribute to the quantitative significance of this effect, but also the frictions within such a system are partly endogenous to the process. Clearly there are many *external* frictions involved in any process of deindustrialisation or reindustrialisation such that labour, plant and equipment will not immediately be taken up by new firms, even in a situation where there is potential demand for such capacity. However, new production will often be averse to moving into areas where old production has moved out because of the characteristics of the labour force. This may in part be that the skills of such a labour force are inappropriate to the new production. But this is unlikely to be the whole explanation. For the same reason that production left, production will not be brought back: capital is seeking a malleable, unorganised, easily controlled group of workers and therefore prefers new, unorganised, industrial workers in new areas, or women in the older areas. This sort of response usually means that workers have to move to the jobs rather than jobs being moved to the workers and thus accentuate all the rigidities imposed by the social infrastructure. Forcing the migration of individual workers contributes to the aims of the employer, but at great social cost. The removal of stagnation becomes conditional on such disintegration. Of course, as a result of this process, other areas are being industrialised so that the net loss in income is determined by the output of workers in the industrialising areas prior to the switch in production, assuming the output of the product they are moving to remains unchanged.

The second characteristic we focus on is the form of integration of the international economy. The growth of international firms means that stagnationist tendencies generated in any one country, by any one or combination of the processes previously analysed, will be immediately transmitted across many countries, and will eventually lead to feedbacks on the originating country. The development of transnational production patterns will tend to speed up and amplify an international stagnationist tendency. Thus an integrated world economy is produced but without an *overall* planning mechanism and yet with an international system of planning operating within each of its major constituent parts. Thus rather than having the stability which could result from international integration within a supra-national planning authority operating at the macroeconomic level across national economies, we have the growing instability of international integration organised by individual transnational corporations.

Perhaps the most vivid example of the integration of the world economy within the capitalist system resulting in a heightened degree of instability is the world financial system. Over recent history, with increasing liberalisation and the diffusion of advanced information technology, the system has become almost completely and immediately integrated. The outcome has been enormous instability induced by international currency speculation. The resulting huge short-term gyrations in exchange rates has undermined the ability of industrial capitalism to plan its investment and production policies and make informed locational decisions. The outcome has been sharp cutbacks in investment in tradeable goods because of the substantial increase in the degree of uncertainty surrounding such investment decisions. The central point is that the very flexibility of unregulated financial capital has induced this state of affairs where the efficiency of industrial capital is greatly impaired. But clearly this is not a matter simply of flexibility, but one of unregulated flexibility. Whilst the transnational banks and financial institutions, and indeed the transnational industrial corporations who are also major actors in currency markets, are operating globally to maximise their returns, national governments have little control over the process. The recent phenomenal growth of the Eurocurrency market, with a size now measured in *trillions* of dollars, has decisively altered the balance of power and international commercial banks emerged as a main focus of financial power, largely independent of the control of national monetary authorities (see Bhaduri and Steindl (1983), p. 7).

We have identified various ways in which the growth of the dominance of transnational corporations may accentuate stagnationist tendencies already endemic within monopoly capitalism. But have we overstated the case? Is it not true that some of the characteristics of these giant organisations militate against such tendencies? Surely the additional flexibility of the transnational is a good, and not a bad, in terms of allowing the rapid, adaptation of the world economy to new conditions? And surely also, these giants act to diffuse new products and new processes more rapidly through the world economic system and thereby maintain a considerable dynamic within that system? Let's try to disentangle these two propositions.

In considering the effect of the flexibility of the basic production unit on the aggregate level of economic activity within a capitalist economic system, it is clear that a certain amount of flexibility is going to be a good thing. Steindl (1966), for example, suggests that the existence of diversified giant corporations allows for the ready diversion of funds from monopolising to competitive sectors of the economy, and thus tends to sustain the rate of investment. But the significance of this process depends on the bounds of the system in terms of democratic control. Economics normally deals with nation-states in which case a sharp distinction has to be drawn between flexibility *within* the nation-state compared with flexibility *between* nation-states. This raises the issue of the transnational and its flexibility which appears *qualitatively* different from that of the purely domestic firm. But this has arisen because we have chosen to focus on the nation-state. Similar issues arise for communities within nation-states; for villages, towns, cities, regions, the optimality of the flexibility of giant firms takes on a very different perspective. To enable communities to determine their own futures requires that they achieve some control over the flexibility of those who provide the jobs. Firms have to be accountable to the community within which they operate. Without it economies and communities will eventually stagnate as a consequence of their development, except for those parts of the key cities of the world where the controllers of such firms choose to locate.

Turning to the possible contribution of the transnationals to the dynamics of the system as a result of their innovatory activity, we can readily agree that major innovations can certainly tend to nullify otherwise stagnationist tendencies. Two questions arise: the first one relates to whether or not the evolution of the dominance of giant transnationals has contributed positively to the development of such innovations; the second one relates to the impact of such innovations on this evolution. On the first point an analysis of the available evidence suggests that technological progressiveness will not normally be promoted by the monopolisation of the system of production (see, for example, Scherer (1980) and Stoneman (1983) for surveys). Despite controlling most of the recorded research and development, the giant corporations have not provided the origins of the major technological innovations. These are often appropriated from much smaller firms, or even individuals, and in many cases their innovation is suppressed or delayed (see, for example, Mandel (1968)). However the transnational organisation of production does mean that once innovation does take place, then international diffusion should rapidly follow. But we must keep clear the purposes and consequences of such diffusion. The innovation of new products by these firms is an attempt to secure and enhance their market positions and hence will contribute to the general tendency for the degree of monopoly to increase over time. Thus while in the short term such innovations may give a boost to investment, in the longer term they constitute a force contributing to the stagnationist trend. Similarly with process innovations. Although those who control the transnationals will be motivated by the search for efficient techniques, this will include the 'efficiency' provided by control over the workforce. Thus new technology will tend to reflect the search for control, which will inevitably have distributional implications favouring profits over wages. In addition there will be a bias embedded in the new technology favouring a system of production and control suited to the transnational giant. Thus process innovations will tend to sustain a monopolisation trend and a distributional trend both of which contribute to the stagnationist tendency previously described. It would therefore appear that to reverse such a tendency requires an accelerating rate of innovation, whether product or process, and there is little indication that a monopolising system has such a capability.

NOTES

1. See, for example, Steindl (1952), Baran and Sweezy (1966), and Cowling (1982). Although Kalecki (1971) provided most of the key theoretical constructions which underpinned these speculations he was never dogmatic about such tendencies.
2. Taking the simplest possible example we assume gross national income comprises profits and wages, and gross national product comprises gross investment, capitalist consumption and worker consumption. We also assume workers receive only wages and do not save. Then it is clear that profits equal gross investment plus capitalist consumption. The interpretation is that the expenditure of capitalists in aggregate determines the level of their profits. Capitalists can individually decide on their level of expenditure but they cannot do this for their level of profits. Kalecki (1971) gives a full theoretical explanation of the determinants of profits, and Cowling (1982) examines the process within the institutions of monopoly capitalism.
3. At the present time, given the enormous destruction wrought by deflationary policies within Britain, there is some movement the other way present across a whole range of political parties. However what is most significant about such movements is the limited nature of their recovery programmes given the enormity of the unemployment problem. There can be no doubt that the political agenda has been decisively changed compared with the earlier post-World War II period.
4. Some will argue that a slump in demand will induce price-cutting which will in turn reduce the degree of monopoly and thus remove the initial cause of the slump in demand. It may be conjectured that the initial impact of a substantial fall in demand may cause an oligopoly group to fly apart. Each member of the group observes that its own sales have dropped and assumes that its rivals have been engaged in price-cutting, or similar market share-augmenting strategies. It therefore responds with similar strategies. However, if the explanation for the original observation is in fact a general slump in demand this will gradually

become more obvious to each member of the group. Faced with such mutual adversity we may anticipate that the group will tend to come together to solve its mutual problems. Thus the initial impact of the turn-down in demand may well be a reduction in price–cost margins. But if the slump persists we can expect to see a recovery in margins as the degree of cooperation or collusion within the oligopoly groups increases. Evidence for this sort of behaviour has become available in the 1970s for the UK (see Cowling, 1983) and Norway (see Berg, 1986).

The existence of a transnational production base itself contributes to the tendency for prices to be held in periods of recession. A recession in one country can lead to plant closure in that country, with the market being sourced from foreign plants. *Without* control of foreign production facilities firms may be forced to operate domestic plants at inefficient rates of output, were the degree of monopoly to be maintained. Thus the growth of transnational firms allows for the more flexible adjustment of production to falling demand and thereby serves to hold price levels when otherwise they may have fallen. A recent detailed study of price formation in British industry supports the view that demand appears in general to have little impact (see Sawyer, 1983).

5. Again the position of Japan is an exception, but increasingly an accommodation is being sought with major United States and European corporations setting up a variety of joint venture arrangements.

6. The description of the nineteenth century comes from Krause and Nye (1975).

7. Whilst this term has been popularised by Fröbel, Heinrichs and Kreye (1981), the basis of the analysis was laid by Adam (1975). Hymer (1972) also has contributed much to the analysis of these tendencies.

8. This is not meant to deny the enormous growth of investment flows between the advanced industrial countries. To the extent to which this is symmetric then it offers no explanation of deindustrialisation. Asymmetries can be due to differences on the demand side or on the supply side. (We consider the demand side later.) A particularly important example of an emerging asymmetry has been the case of the UK and its European neighbours, with production for the UK market being increasingly located within the rest of Europe, to a substantial degree by British or United States corporations.

9. For an analysis of the changing spatial structures of production within the UK, see Massey (1984).

10. In some cases the production unit supplying the services will be large-scale, but still in some sense subordinate. For example it could be argued that the publicly-owned British Leyland was maintained by state subsidy to supply assembly services to the (dominant) component producers. Similarly the public utilities, under the prescription of marginal cost pricing, could be seen in a similar relationship to the industrial users of their services.

11. The independent producers could be workers' cooperatives. Rather than workers being exploited within the sphere of production or

distribution, under these arrangements the exploitation would come via the market for the product.

12. Whilst the climate may have something to do with this movement, the use of such terms tends to shift the focus away from the fundamental explanation which lies in the conflict between capital and labour.

13. Detailed calculations on these points are contained in Dowrick (1983).

14. This does not undermine the previous suggestion that the growth of the small business sector is being supported by the giants. That part of the small business sector which is seen as complementary by the giants we can expect to be financed.

15. A survey by the *Financial Times* (21 October 1982) revealed that no less than 25 of the top 50 corporations in Europe are British-based.

16. They indeed accept that for the foreign-controlled firms most of the new jobs were simply due to acquisitions. They also point out that the dichotomy between British transnationals and British domestic firms was by no means clear-cut. Many of the 'domestics' had considerable foreign holdings.

17. This reveals the interdependence of our arguments. We have argued that, in a transnational world, worker militancy leads to deindustrialisation but, in turn, these processes feed back on the labour market and tend to depress the power of labour and thus reduce wage costs.

18. There will be exceptions. The positions of strategic staff at the core of these giant firms will not be eroded by transnationalism – indeed the empires which they control will be constantly augmented by the evolution of transnationalism.

19. These issues will be further analysed in the next chapter.

6 Democracy, Planning and the Transnationals

We have described a world in which the dominance of the transnationals has advanced considerably in recent history and we have analysed some of the major economic consequences. We see the transnationals as having played a key role in the unravelling of the implications of the monopoly capitalist system in terms of a distributional tendency favouring profits which in turn implies an underlying tendency to stagnation. Within these general tendencies the growth of transnationalism has imposed deindustrialisation on the older industrialised nations and unregulated industrial growth on others. The growth of such power raises many issues, but the fundamental one is that of the ability of people, and the communities of which they are part, to assert their right to determine their own future. This is the essence of democracy. Fundamental to maximising a community's economic welfare is economic democracy: the ability of people and their communities to allocate resources in the way they choose. This can be portrayed in terms of a community's welfare function with income distribution and allocative efficiency as arguments. This function is maximised when the community makes its own choices: if others make the choices they will impose their wishes and therefore choose the allocation which suits them – there is no reason why this should correspond to the community's optimum and every reason why it should differ, simply because resources are scarce and therefore the decision-maker can gain at the expense of others. There is a further justification for democracy – it may well enter the welfare function as a separate argument. This would not, of course, *per se* imply the presence of full democracy.

In theory, this requirement for economic democracy fits very easily within neoclassical economics since the neoclassical view is all about individuals making their choices. In practice it cuts across the grain of neoclassical analysis which assumes an even distribution of power, thus ignores power asymmetries and therefore fails to grasp the democratic/ undemocratic distinction – its very essence is normally assumed away. (See, for instance, the discussion of voluntary exchange, a tenet of neoclassicism, in Chapter 2; this gives everyone the right of veto, nobody the power to force another into a worse position.)

To begin to achieve economic democracy people and communities must possess some significant degree of direct control over the dominant centres of economic power. Underlying this requirement is the fundamental asymmetry between the locational mobility of the transnational corporation in terms of its production and investment strategies and the locational rigidity or inflexibility of people in general, and their communities. This implies a basic asymmetry of power which can only be curbed by direct intervention by communities, nation-states or groups of nation-states in the activities of the transnationals. The asymmetry described is simply an extension of the more general one which exists between communities and capital. The mobility of capital gives it power over cities, regions and nations, and imposes a requirement for political democracy in order to gain economic democracy. The giant transnational simply embodies such power to the nth degree: international flexibility is a crucial added dimension to inter-regional flexibility. Size adds to such power; giving great power even without significant mobility, for example the power to determine how markets are allowed to work and the environment within which they operate. Communities can respond to such power by combination when facing employers; and by representative government. But transnationalism allows an escape from such countervailing power, which in turn has to be countered. This chapter will first examine the basic democratic issues, starting with a broad perspective and then focusing on the contemporary issues raised by the dominance of the transnationals.[1] We then identify institutions and mechanisms aimed at securing democratic control and bringing the system back to full employment and efficient growth. These will include measures to limit and control existing centres of economic power – the major corporations, and initiatives aimed at the growth out of the existing system of an alternative system based on democratic planning.

DEMOCRACY AND CAPITALISM

There are some who argue that only under capitalism is democracy feasible. One of the most recent exponents of this view argues that democracy is protected by entrusting the economy with the assignment of income, occupations and authority on the grounds of the intrinsic instability of democracy (see Usher, 1981). If we are interested in preserving democracy then we should not lightly tamper with the economy or the outcome of the economic system. For democracy to survive there must be a prior agreement among citizens on a set of rules of assignment – a system of equity – and capitalism contains a system of equity sufficient to permit democracy to continue.

The basic problem with this view is that it focuses exclusively on the significance of the independence of the assignment mechanism from the political arena – a degree of independence sufficient to allow democratic government to proceed, but ignores the question of the dependence of the political arena on the assignment mechanism (system of equity). In reality the form of political democracy is not fully determined by the system of voting, but also by the distribution of economic power, part of which will be devoted to gaining the consent of the majority. It is also important to emphasise that capitalism existed for extended periods without allowing democracy even to start, and in many places within the capitalist ambit it still does not exist even in the limited form we experience in this country.[2] On this point it is interesting to note that Usher argues that the economic conditions for universal franchise have been achieved only in this century. He favours Cromwell's position in the Putney debates during the English revolution – property qualifications for voting are necessary because property is indispensable for the maintenance of civilised society, and the institution of property can be preserved only if the poor are prevented from voting it out of existence. Thus the preservation of democracy, conditional on the preservation of property, implies that democracy has a variable meaning since the conditions needed to preserve it imply a diminution in the institution itself as well as in its role. It would appear that the original aim of choosing a form of economic organisation which would secure democracy has been replaced by the aim of securing the form of economic organisation itself, with its existing unequal distribution of power. Such inequality is seen as desirable for reasons of dynamic efficiency: without it accumulation would falter. The old, conservative argument reappears – don't worry about how the cake is divided, just notice its size and rate of growth! Whether this is a compelling *economic* argument will be considered later. What seems to be asserted is the primacy of economic efficiency over democracy. What is desirable is that degree of democracy which is consistent with the prerogative of property, which is required for economic efficiency. All talk of a form of economic organisation consistent with stable democracy is at best secondary.

Despite the variable meaning given to democracy by Usher, the one constant feature is the lack of participation. This echoes the view of much of contemporary political theory and political sociology. Political equality is then simply equated with universal suffrage. Participation is ruled out by 'the facts of political life' – the problems of scale in modern industrial society and the apathy of its citizens. It is also seen to be undesirable because of the instability it would create – the experience of Weimar Germany is cited, as is the then generally observed lack of attachment to democracy of the apathetic masses who would be asked to participate. As Lively (1975) points out, the unspoken assumption is that stability is impossible at a greater level of democracy than is currently observed, and indeed that what is being stabilised is itself desirable. All this is in sharp contrast to those theorists who give a deeper meaning to political equality and require participation by the people in all aspects of society as a precondition of democracy. Rousseau saw economic equality and economic independence as necessary preconditions for political equality; participation ensured political equality was made effective. The greater the participation of the individual, the better able she is to do so. John Stuart Mill also saw participation as providing 'good' government but also better individuals. He also came to see the importance of participation in the workplace, but it was G. D. H. Cole who developed more fully the idea of participatory democracy in a modern industrial society. For democracy to exist a participatory society must exist, not simply for its direct contribution to democracy via participation within that particular sphere of activity – for example, the workplace – but also because of the indirect effect on the democratic process in general. Eliminating authoritarianism in one sphere contributes to its elimination elsewhere. This also means that greater democracy within the political arena would be expected to lead to demands for democracy elsewhere. If this is not forthcoming then stable democracy is not possible, assuming congruence is not achieved by less democracy in government! It would suggest however that 'greater participation would enhance rather than detract from the stability of economic regimes' (Lively (1975), p.86). The fact of ignorance, apathy and alienation is not an argument *against* participation, but for it.

Extending participation within the workplace is therefore of crucial significance for democracy in its broadest sense, but it is precisely at this point that the incompatibility between democracy and capitalism emerges. Equal participation of all involved in an economic enterprise would undermine the essence of a capitalist firm. It is not the market which is the essence of a capitalist system – a feature which tends to be emphasised by those equating capitalism with freedom and democracy – since it is possible to envisage a non-capitalist market system consisting of independent producers or workers' cooperatives. Rather it is the subordination of wage labour within the production process. Whilst some degree of participation by workers in decision-making within the capitalist enterprise will always be present it can never approach the level of *equal* participation without transforming social relations within the firm. Again this does not mean that non-capitalist production cannot exist within a capitalist system, rather the point is that non-capitalist production cannot be dominant without transforming such a system.

We should also be clear that within a representative political democracy, as is the case for most advanced industrial countries, participation will include intervention by government within the strategic planning of the major capitalist enterprises as well as democratising decision-making within the specific operational units. There are two basic reasons why this will normally be seen as necessary: first, because the collective interests of the population at large will need to be secured in the presence of these major centres of economic power, whether such power is held by specific capitalist groupings or jointly by capitalist and worker; and second, because it will often, in practice, not be feasible for workers and their representatives to capture a significant power base in terms of strategic decision-making by giant firms with a global reach. A well-functioning democracy is always likely to contain at least these two levels of participation and therefore will require the setting-up of institutions and mechanisms to allow for the efficient articulation of policy-making between the two. We shall consider these matters later.

Thus full democracy implies equal participation for all, in all aspects of society, and capitalism must deny this within the economic arena.[3] A fundamental antagonism therefore exists between capitalism and democracy, an antagonism which is obscured by the existence of universal suffrage. This does not mean that the winning of universal suffrage was not a significant gain in the march towards a full democracy, nor that further gains cannot be made within the capitalist system. It suggests rather that further gains will be strongly resisted and that ultimately further democratic advance will require a transformation in the system. Some may argue we already have a 'mixed economy', with the public sector assuming an important role, so that the system is already transformed. Without getting into detailed argument, it seems clear that capitalist enterprise retains an important (and we would argue dominant) position in the economy and that public enterprise has retained a form of work organisation as authoritarian as that of the capitalist sector, so that the existence of a 'mixed economy' appears, as yet, to have had only a limited impact on the democratic polity. Nevertheless, public ownership has undoubtedly given government at least the potential for securing greater leverage over strategic economic choices and to that extent implies an extension of democratic control within the economic system.

GREATER ECONOMIC CONCENTRATION – DECLINING DEMOCRACY

Whilst the incompatibility of democracy with the capitalist organisation of production is a feature of any capitalist system, the incompatibility is particularly marked as economic power becomes more concentrated. Equal participation within the economic enterprise will always be inconsistent with capitalism, but so long as capitalist enterprise remains small-scale its power to subvert the system of democracy remains circumscribed. Clearly, so long as any degree of economic inequality exists then political equality will generally not exist, but the *extent* of political inequality will be related to the *degree* of economic inequality. The evolution of capitalism has led to the growth in the concentration of control over economic resources. As a result many people have lost their economic independence and therefore some degree of control over their own lives, others have had some degree of autonomy taken away from them, and centres of economic power have grown up which are capable of subverting the political process. As an index of concentration within, for example, the United Kingdom, consider the share of the 100 largest enterprises in manufacturing net output. In 1909 the top 100 firms had a 16 per cent share, which rose to 22 per cent in 1949, 32 per cent in 1958 and 42 per cent in 1975 (see Aaronovitch and Smith, 1981). Estimates of the share of the 100 largest quoted industrial and commercial companies in terms of net assets reveals a figure of 47 per cent in 1948, rising to 64 per cent in 1968 and 80 per cent in 1976. There is every indication that the British economy is increasingly dominated by a relatively few firms; similar results have been obtained for other advanced industrial countries.[4] We should also remember that the measures of concentration used will tend to understate the true position because no account is taken of the interrelationships between firms of a minority or informal kind, such as common shareholders, interlocking directorates or joint ventures, together with the links through the market which we have described in Chapter 2.

But growth in sheer size is not the only threat to democratic control; parallel changes in the organisation of big business will also tend to undermine democracy. The two related tendencies which stand out in this regard are transnationalism and centripetal developments. At one and the same time the dominant centres of economic power, the major corporations, are internationalising production and drawing the control of the use of an ever increasing share of the world's economic resources into the ambit of the key cities of the world. These twin developments pose problems for the democratic control of work and the strategy of the firm, for democratic control within the evolution of the city or region, and ultimately undermine the autonomy of the nation-state itself.

Take transnationalism first. The constant theme of this book has been the extent to which production and markets are increasingly controlled by giant corporations with a transnational base. Again, this is not simply a matter of the ownership of production facilities in many different countries, although this is an extremely important development with much of the world's trade being conducted between the affiliates of the same organisation (see Chapter 2 and 3), but also links across countries which are dominated by the giant corporations without a significant degree of ownership. This would include various forms of subcontracting, franchising, licensing and joint venture arrangements. Given such emerging international control of production and markets, and given the progressive reductions in national and international controls over trade and capital flows, the leverage of the giant corporations over the individual nation-state has been considerably increased. Democratic national decisions to control the activities of the major corporations, or to tax them, have been and will be increasingly circumvented by the appropriate international reallocation of production and trade flows (or merely by the *threat* of such reallocation), accompanied by appropriate transfer-pricing policies. At the same time, the increased international competition for investment and jobs created by the existence of international firms which can flexibly reallocate production and investment, and accentuated in the current world economic crisis, have forced and will tend to force nation-states in the absence of a fundamental change in strategy, to reduce corporate taxation and the regulation of production, increase the subsidisation of investment and employment, and act to restrain, by government action, the growth of wage costs. As identified in the previous chapter, such restraint will eventually incorporate a shift in the macroeconomic policy stance of government. Keynesianism, whilst congruent with the interests of capital at certain periods of history, will eventually be dropped in favour of supply-side policies aimed at controlling the growth of real wages.

Thus, while we might expect the advent of universal suffrage to lead to demands for the redistribution of income, wealth and power in favour of the majority, coupled with government intervention in the macroeconomy aimed at securing full employment, the existence of giant transnational centres of economic power will undermine such democratic demands. Indeed we can see the growth of transnationalism as partly a response to the problems posed for the giant corporations by the advent of greater political democracy coupled with the rising power and militancy of labour, and the result will not only be the attenuation of the significance of such political institutions, but also a tendency to undermine the growth in the institutions themselves. The provision of investment and jobs is being made conditional on the suppression of progressive forces which would allow the growth of economic and political self-determination. This is perhaps most vividly seen in Latin America, but it is a general tendency.

The other characteristics of central importance for democratic control, which arise with the growth of giant corporations, are the underlying centripetal tendencies within such organisations. Within the advanced industrial countries the giant firm has emerged largely as a result of merger activity (see, for example, Prais, 1976). Large numbers of small firms have, over sometimes extended periods of time, become agglomerated into large multi-plant firms. As an example of this process at work, Prais reports that the number of plants controlled by 100 largest manufacturing enterprises in the United Kingdom rose from an average of 27 in 1958 to an average of 72 in 1972 and this was largely the result of the acquisition of other firms by the giants. This sort of transformation of the industrial structure of this country and others has, in many cases, led to the loss of a degree of local and regional autonomy, and in some cases where the acquirer is a foreign-based corporation, a loss of national autonomy. This is not to say the system of relatively small firms, with a local base, which characterised the earlier industrial structure represented a thriving democracy in microcosm; but there was nevertheless an element of local control which disappeared following merger. Higher-level decision-making and associated higher-level occupations have been pulled to the centre and the periphery has developed all the characteristics of a branch plant economy. Strategic decisions with major implications for many local, regional and national communities are being made elsewhere.[5] For an increasing proportion of people control over their lives is being eroded by such centralising economic forces. But not only is local autonomy being reduced. The same centralising forces imply a siphoning-off of resources to the centre, which reduces the capacity of the periphery to sustain its own economic, political and cultural development on which future self-determination is based. For a largely autonomous local, regional or national economy, not only will the community receive the wage and salary share of the income generated, but most of the profit share as well. As the economic base of the area is taken over by outside interests, so the profit share is extracted for use at the centre and lost to the local community. Now of course it was always the case that only a small fraction of the community had a direct claim on the profit share, and it is also the case that at least part of the profit share after takeover will be returned for investment. Nevertheless it was probably generally true that the philanthropy of the local rich made a contribution to the cultural development of the local community which has been lost in the centralising process.[6] Generally the growth of economic dependency has stunted the broader development of a local, regional or national community and therefore imperilled its future hopes of self-determination.

Thus democratic control suffers in two respects: control over higher-level decisions is being lost, as is control over the resources required for community self-determination. The almost inevitable outcome is the outmigration of the educated, leading to further decline in the cultural development of the community. Centripetal economic tendencies become centripetal political and cultural tendencies and the community enters a vicious circle of relative decline. Thus whole communities lose effective control over their own lives – the essence of true democracy. It is also the case that such communities cannot easily break out of such processes of cumulative causation by supply-side adjustments, such as investing in education – which might be a typical, democratic response, so long as the demand side remains outside their control. If such supply adjustments are made, the most likely outcome would be a speeding-up of the rate of out-migration and thus an increase in the rate of relative decline. Increasing educational investment will only effectively contribute to the economic and cultural resurgence of the community if parallel action is taken to secure control of production, employment and investment. We shall develop this point later in the context of our discussion of industrial policy.

GREATER DEMOCRACY MEANS BETTER ECONOMIC PERFORMANCE

In raising the question of the extension of democracy into the economy the orthodox view would be that there is some trade-off between democracy and economic efficiency – both are desirable but to get more of the one we have to give up some of the other. We believe this view to be incorrect, and therefore we do not see that creating the required conditions for better economic performance need get in the way of greater democracy – in fact, just the reverse. In establishing a greater degree of democratic control within and over the major centres of economic power the objectives of better economic performance will also be realised.

As a perhaps extreme illustration of this proposition let us reconsider the origins of the present deep slump of the British economy and then a democratic response to it. As we observed in Chapter 5, three interacting tendencies have been at work: the general movement of the world economy into slump; the growing *relative* weakness of the British economy, and the move by successive recent British governments away from Keynesian demand management. It can be argued that all three tendencies have arisen because of an inadequate degree of economic control within the economic system, but we shall put the general stagnationist tendency to one side for later consideration.

As suggested in Chapter 5, the British economy has had a long-term tendency to generate a significantly lower rate of productivity growth compared with rivals. The underlying causes are a matter of considerable controversy, but we have suggested two, partially complementary, explanations warrant attention. One of the significant features of the British economy is the relatively high degree of internationalisation of British capital, both industrial and financial. These strong international links imply that capital can be easily shifted abroad with a consequent retarding effect on investment in Britain (see Aaronovitch and Smith, 1981). This could easily trigger off a cumulative process of relative decline. In contrast, the continental European countries and Japan exploited foreign markets from a domestic production base and entered a cumulative process of relative expansion. But what is it about the British economy that has led British capital to such a peculiarly international orientation? Undoubtedly there are many historical roots, but another view of the determinants of relative decline may offer a partial explanation. This view stresses the peculiar strength and militancy of British labour at the point of production which has retarded innovation and productivity growth (see Kilpatrick and Lawson, 1980). The international orientation of British capital could then be seen as a response, although the converse argument is also made, that the lack of growth of the British economy, due, for example, to its international orientation, has forced workers and their unions into a defensive posture which has retarded the growth process even further (see Currie and Smith, 1981). If Britain's relative economic decline is at least partially explicable in terms of the peculiar strength of labour's workplace organisation, then the extension of democratic control offers the prospect of a transformation of Britain's economic prospects. A defensive posture would be transformed into positive participation if it were clear that those who were participating had effective, economic control over both operating and strategic decisions. This effect would be reinforced by economic control over the transnationals, both industrial and financial, for example by local enterprise boards, by the trustees of pension funds and by national government. Such intervention would imply the introduction of a broader level of participation into the planning of international trade and capital flows currently orchestrated mainly by the giant transnational corporations, and in many cases implying, as in the British case in recent history, an inconsistency with national democratic objectives.

Of course there is another way, and that way is the major project of the present government in the United Kingdom, and, to a perhaps lesser extent, of governments generally within the advanced industrial countries. However, as well as being basically undemocratic in terms of smashing the defensive strength of the organisation of working people within a capitalist system in which there is a huge imbalance of economic power between the great mass of the population and the few who control the major corporations, it is also extremely costly in social terms. This brings us to the third tendency underlying the present slump of the British economy: the progressive movement away from Keynesian demand management we have witnessed since the mid-1970s. As we have already argued (see Chapter 5) a commitment to full employment will have a fundamental impact on the balance of power between capital and labour and will eventually lead, via rising confidence and militancy, to rising wage demands and ultimately a wage-price spiral, which the government will sooner or later seek to clamp down. Incomes policies have been tried and abandoned and eventually some variant of monetarism was wheeled out as a replacement for the old, 'discredited' policies.[7] Clearly the Thatcher government in Britain, and administrations elsewhere, have been acting in a manner aimed at securing labour discipline and, for a period, such policies undoubtedly met with some success. However, they have been gained at enormous cost in terms of unemployment and lost production and their long-term benefits now look dubious.

Is there a better way? The history of incomes policy in the 1960s and 1970s, when it had any impact at all, was one of reducing the growth in real wage. As Burkitt (1982) points out, the state was essentially nationalising part of the product which it then handed over to capitalists. Workers were, in effect, compelled to restrict consumption in order to facilitate investment, yet they possessed no rights in the ensuing accumulation of capital. The issue is even more sharply drawn where production is organised on a transnational basis. Facilitating investment may then mean facilitating the export of capital, which may in turn imply greater competition for jobs. Not surprisingly, workers eventually baulked at this and the system of wage control broke down. At the same time it is clear that wage militancy by itself, within a system of transnational monopoly capitalism, cannot secure a permanent redistribution of income between capital and labour – a much deeper penetration of monopoly capitalism is required. Thus labour has a strong interest in a prices and incomes policy, as one mode of achieving this; but a necessary precondition is the increasing socialisation of capital. However, it is not sufficient that workers' holdings of equity should increase directly through individual shareholdings or indirectly via the growth of pension funds. What matters is the control of capital. Workers' individual holdings will inevitably be too diffuse and their pension funds are typically controlled by their employers and indirectly by the highly concentrated institutions of financial capital (see Minns, 1980). Effective control will only come with collective share ownership and institutional changes in the way pension funds are managed. The growth in pension funds in particular is of enormous importance for labour if control can be established over the use of such funds. The socialisation of capital implies not simply an extension of communal ownership of capital, but also an extension of economic democracy – worker involvement and representation in all areas and all levels of decision-making within the enterprise. Only in such circumstances is the abandonment of free collective bargaining likely to be a stable solution.

But it will be argued that giving the workers more say in the organisation and operation of industry will mean that industry will suffer in terms of loss of efficiency and loss of dynamism. It is one thing talking about increased economic democracy, but that's so much ivory towered nonsense! Not so. All the evidence points to the real gains which can be obtained by democratising the place of work. A survey in 1970 of the existing empirical research on participation concluded that not only did it have a favourable effect on the development of the individual but that it did not harm the efficiency of the enterprise, indeed it may have increased it (Pateman, 1970). A more recent survey went further and concluded that there is 'overwhelming evidence that increased participation ... raises productivity' (Hodgson, 1984). In the case of workers' cooperatives, the empirical evidence reveals that participation increases workers' self-discipline; fewer resources are devoted to supervision compared with capitalist firms; and absenteeism dropped significantly following the introduction of worker control, with absenteeism in the Mondragon cooperatives only half that of the capitalist firms in the region (Stewart, 1983).

But it is not simply a matter of participation at the level of the production process and within the operational decision-making of the individual plant. We also require an extension of democratic control over the strategic decisions of the major corporations. The aim of any (for example, national) community is to create a dynamic and productive (national) economy and the private strategic decision-making of the major corporations may not be consistent with this. In the specific case of the British economy at this stage of its development two features stand out as major encumbrances – the relatively short-run perspective of the financial institutions and the global perspective of the major corporations in general, whether British or foreign-owned (see, for example, Aaronovitch and Smith, 1981). It may be in the private interests of the

City to be obsessive about short-term profitability, although we are inclined to doubt it; it will also be natural for giant corporations to seek to minimise their costs by choosing least-cost production locations wherever they may occur throughout the world. But it is the responsibility of the national community to intervene to secure a longer-term perspective in certain strategic areas of economic decision-making and also ensure that the national interest is reflected in the global strategy of those transnational corporations which choose to sell their product in the national market. The fundamental issue, as we have stated already, is that capital is highly mobile and flexible whereas most people and communities are not.

Whilst the penetration by labour of decision-making within the corporation will serve to bend the strategy of the corporation towards that of the national community there are two reasons for suggesting that intervention by national government will also be required. First, it is clear that meaningful participation within the enterprise will, beyond a certain point, be strongly resisted – the organised response by the transnationals to the minimal requirements of the Vredeling Directive (prepared by the EEC Commission) is a recent case in point. Thus even given the coincidence of the interests of workers within a specific enterprise and the broader community, intervention by national government will certainly be necessary wherever full participation has not been achieved and such full participation is made especially difficult where production has a transnational base. Politically we may see the evolution of governments willing and able to intervene decisively in the strategic decision-making of the major corporations before we see full participation by workers within the specific enterprise. The second point is that the aims of a specific group of workers may not be fully congruent with those of the community so that even with full participation within the enterprise the intervention by government in strategic decision-making would still be required. This is most likely to occur in cases where monopoly power is substantial.

We have referred to the British example as an extreme case where the short-run perspective of the financial institutions and the global perspective of the dominant corporations are seen as particular impediments to the evolution of a successful national economy, but the reasons for intervention are completely general. National or regional communities, given their almost definitional immobility, will always tend to adopt a longer-term national perspective than will the transnational corporation. Equally the global strategy of the transnationals can be inimical to national economic development in all countries. At certain stages of their development some countries will see investment by the transnationals as congruent with their interests and, in a limited sense, it may well be. But this does not dispose of the fundamental argument that the flexibility of such investment will *generally* act against the economic evolution of such countries. The answer to issues of poverty, unemployment and lack of development is not transnational planning by the major corporations, but national planning within such economies. The transnationals act to plan production *within sectors* of the global economy whereas national planning is concerned with planning *across sectors* within a nation. Thus planning by the transnationals will tend to ignore matters of imbalance or disruption within any location, while national planning seeks balance and lack of disruption within any country (see Hymer, 1972). We leave the detailed discussion of an alternative system of strategic planning to the next section.

The argument in this section has been that an extension of democracy will contribute to rather than detract from the performance of the economic system and we have interpreted the extension of democracy as both a fuller participation by workers within the economic enterprise together with a greater degree of intervention by the government, within the so-called market system. At this point a more fundamental issue is raised. At the core of orthodox economics lies the notion of consumer sovereignty. Ultimate power or control lies within the individual household. The producer, for example the transnational corporation, responds to the expressed desires of consumers via the market. Consumer equilibrium is reached when satisfaction cannot be raised by any further reallocation of expenditures among competing goods and services. The consumer has certain preferences and allocates her income among alternatives so as to maximise her utility. If, however, the preferences of the consumer are subject to external management or manipulation, for example via advertising, then the theory of consumer demand has to be rewritten in terms not of the preferences of consumers but of the preferences of those who seek to manage such preferences. Once it is admitted that the wants which the producer is responding to are, at least in part, determined by the producer, then the whole structure of the system is inverted. The new sequence originates within the corporation, with the wants of consumers being created and adapted in the interests of the corporation. This is not to deny the existence of the old sequence within those parts of the economic system peripheral to the monopoly capitalist core. But it is nothing more than that – peripheral.

Whilst in the new sequence the consumer continues to maximise her own utility, the adjustment can be brought about just as easily by the manipulation of preferences by the producer as by the reallocation of her budget by the consumer. Once this sort of intervention is admitted, then the case against other forms of intervention in the microeconomics of the system is no longer as clear as the economic orthodoxy would have us believe. If we are to allow firms the freedom to persuade, then we cannot easily disallow government the means to constrain the individual in her consumption patterns. If the consumer is not sovereign then sovereignty is not taken away from the individual by collective action. Since the system we have been analysing is one in which the expenditure on advertising is enormous, then the fundamental grounds for non-intervention in the market system are insecure. In subscribing to an alternative system of planning to that of the transnationals we need have little fear that we are transgressing individual consumer sovereignty to any greater extent than is already the case. This is not meant to imply that consumer sovereignty is of little concern within an alternative planning system. Rather it is meant to emphasise that *democratic* planning will serve to sustain something which has been increasingly undermined in the course of the development of the monopoly capitalist system.

Lastly we need also to remember that, left to its own devices, the monopoly capitalist system will tend to secular stagnation. Democratic intervention within the macroeconomy has become more important as the economic system has become more concentrated and therefore more prone to stagnation. But such intervention has been undermined in two ways: by the political power of big business in pushing governments away from full employment policies at certain conjunctures and by the reduction in the efficiency of Keynesian-type interventionist policies resulting from the transnational evolution of the organisation of production. As a result the balance of forces has dramatically shifted against the democratic demand for full-employment policies. Although there will inevitably be shifts back to programmes offering a greater commitment to the reduction in unemployment, these are likely to be less dramatic than was true during the long boom so long as the countries involved fail to take decisive action to raise significantly the degree of their own economic autonomy.[8] Without such action Keynesian reflation will be restricted by the immediate and dramatic consequences for the balance of payments; the experience of the French socialist government in the 1980s provides a clear example of what can happen when something more ambitious is attempted without the other necessary measures. We shall explore these measures in the next section.

DEMOCRATIC PLANNING AND TRANSNATIONAL CONTROL

Given the degree to which democracy throughout the world is limited by the lack of economic democracy and the growing concentration of economic power, the significant extension of democracy, and thereby economic efficiency, can only proceed by the democratisation of work and investment decisions, and by increasing the degree of democratic control over the monopolisation of the economy and over the transnational corporations. Thus, in addition to regulating the major corporations and their transnational operations, such a democratic programme will begin to counterpose a system of democratic planning which will increasingly dominate the economic system, whilst not seeking to displace entirely the existing market system. Such a programme will contain mutually reinforcing demand- and supply-side strategies. Not only will the government pursue active short-term demand management policies to ensure a level of aggregate demand consistent with full-employment, but complementary with such policies, supply-side strategies determining the longer-term capacity of the economy will be inaugurated. Within the interstices of such a system the market system will remain. Whilst it cannot be relied on, particularly in a monopoly capitalist world, to generate a level of aggregate demand consistent with full employment, nor can any national or regional community assume that market forces, particularly in a world of dominant transnational (or national) corporations, will ensure the long-term economic viability of that community, nevertheless we would argue the market system remains as a potentially efficient allocational device, when set within the appropriate democratically controlled framework. We would certainly not see democratic planning as getting bogged down in directly determining the myriad complex transactions distinguishing a typical modern economy.

We shall start our analysis by considering demand-side policies aimed at restoring full employment to countries, like those throughout Europe and North America, that have a considerable surplus of unutilised industrial capacity which we have argued has come about, directly or indirectly, via the activities of the dominant transnational corporations. Such policies are therefore to be seen as a response to the *symptoms* of crisis induced by such a system, not the underlying causes. In the course of analysing appropriate demand-side policies, we shall inevitably engage the matter of the *regulation* of transnational power as a necessary condition for securing the desired response to these policies. We shall then turn to longer-term questions on the supply side and spell out what we see as central issues of a democratic industrial strategy to be counterposed to that of the transnationals. Again, the prime focus will be on the advanced industrial countries, but inevitably the analysis will contain much of relevance to newly industrialising countries. We shall be analysing the issues from a national perspective and shall be seeking to establish a greater degree of national economic autonomy which will in turn serve to increase the efficiency of national Keynesian demand management previously discussed. Subsequently we shall consider possible supranational initiatives where linkages can be developed within a new network of relatively autonomous national communities. Thus a democratic international economic system can begin to be constructed from the older order managed by the transnationals.

DEMAND-SIDE STRATEGY

We shall start with a national strategy aimed at securing full employment as rapidly as possible. We shall use the United Kingdom at its current stage of development as an example, although we see this as an extreme example of the general case of the older industrialised capitalist countries. We are simply seeking to illustrate some general propositions within a specific context.

Given that the system is operating well below capacity an appropriate combination of fiscal and monetary expansion could potentially secure a rapid increase in output[9] There is no reason to suppose this could not be achieved at prevailing price and wage levels. Our view of the typical firm would be one characterised by a price structure considerably in excess of marginal costs and operating under more or less constant marginal costs except at close to full capacity working (see Chapter 3). Under these conditions no inducement in terms of a fall in real wage is required to generate an output response to an increase in demand. Profits would increase with output if real wages were held constant, and could still increase if real wages rose. We do not of course know what would happen to the price structure with expansionary policies without price control, although given the large gap between current and capacity output we would not expect much of an *extra* increase for even quite substantial increases in demand. The basic point is that we would expect a strong output response to any expansion in demand which is seen to be more than transient.[10] The stronger the commitment the stronger the output response we might expect. Similarly with employment. Given the recent dramatic shake-outs of labour a sustained increase in output in the short term could not be achieved without an increase in hours or employment of production workers. If employers are uncertain about the increase in demand, or whether it will be sustained, they will prefer an adjustment in hours rather than employment. Uncertainty can be reduced by making clear the commitment to full employment and sustained expansion, but incentives could usefully be added to secure a rapid turn-around.[11] Thus *incremental* employment could be subsidised whilst making clear that the level of subsidy will fall with the fall in unemployment. The subsidy could, given the existing burden of unemployment, be substantial so long as it was directed at the increment in employment rather than frittered away on the total, for example via a reduction in pay-roll taxes which would probably have little impact, except on profits. The main point is that measures should be aimed directly at the problem rather than spread generally and relying on the trickle-down hypothesis. That is, get the macro-stance right, then direct expenditure and controls at securing full employment as rapidly as possible.

What sort of expansion are we talking about? With 15 per cent unemployment the increase in output would be about 25 per cent, if (a) constant marginal production costs prevail; (b) production workers are about 60 per cent of total labour; and (c) hours of work are constant.[12] But it is likely that less productive plants would be restarted or expanded, so let us assume, as a rough approximation, that an output expansion of 20 per cent would be required for full employment.[13] Is this possible in the short term, say over two or three years? Although it would require an urgency of approach and a fair amount of planning we don't see why not. Historically, such expansion has not been observed in the United Kingdom, although it is not unknown elsewhere: but neither have we observed such enormous reserves of unutilised capacity in recent history. Note also that the US economy achieved an expansion of 75 per cent in industrial production over a three-year period of World War II, and despite being deprived of much of its skilled manpower. Of course, the whole programme can be undermined, from a national perspective, by the transnationals choosing to source the British expansion from overseas plants. We shall examine this question, along with other problems, in the next section.

PROBLEMS AND CONSTRAINTS

Imports

The question arises if demand is stimulated by a combination of fiscal and monetary measures, how can we be sure that this will not immediately be siphoned off in an expansion of imports and a subsequent deterioration in the balance of trade. To some extent the problem would be self-correcting because the commitment to expansion by the British government would probably lead to a depreciation of the currency and would therefore go some way in mitigating the present lack of competitiveness of British manufacturing. This process could be extended by reducing the British rate of interest. But this issue should not be addressed simply by focusing on the exchange rate. Whilst a significant depreciation of sterling will have a beneficial effect on British manufacturing output, it will also have other less attractive features. The price of food and raw materials will inevitably rise, with undesirable consequences for inflation and the distribution of income. This could be countered in various ways, but it may be more convenient to introduce import controls on a range of strategic manufactured goods rather then a general devaluation. This should not be seen as an attempt to isolate Britain from the international community, but part of an attempt to replace the private planning of trade by the dominant transnational corporations by social planning. The aim will be to restore the manufacturing base of the British economy in order to allow it to grow at a much faster rate than it otherwise would have been able to, and in the process to provide a bigger market for the rest of the world economy.[14]

More needs to be said about the mechanisms of adjustment to exchange rate changes in a world where transnational corporations control a substantial proportion of trade flows. With an appreciation in the currency, as occurred during the early Thatcher years, the transnational will have an incentive to source the domestic market from some foreign affiliate and as a result import-penetration will increase. Whilst this may result in a price decline this is not necessarily the outcome – the oligopoly group may continue to cluster around the old price. A price-cut may be seen as an aggressive act warranting a sharp response. Such a threat would tend to stabilise the group at an existing price. If this were so, then the degree of monopoly (p/mc) for the transnational will have risen and there is an extra incentive to raise the level of advertising and thereby the market share of importers. The outcome would be that whilst the price of imports had *not* fallen import penetration would have *increased*. Whilst this is only a theoretical possibility it would appear to be empirically highly observable. Consider the case of the British car market. The period of significant appreciation for the pound in the early 1980s witnessed the emergence of a huge gap between prices for cars *generally* in Britain and on the Continent and with the subsequent depreciation of sterling the gap has narrowed.[15]

The general point is this: there can be no presumption that, in the case of manufactured goods with a domestic production base, price will either fall with an appreciating currency or rise with a depreciating one. Nevertheless, imports will grow or decline in such cases, and therefore unemployment will be raised or lowered, without such changes impacting on the real wage. Thus the possible disadvantages of exchange rate depreciation are minimised in a world of transnational corporations operating in oligopolistic markets. Where there is no domestic production base, for example in the case of some manufactures, but many raw materials, we would be more likely to observe price sensitivity to the real exchange rate. This would suggest that trade policy should focus more directly on the problem – that is, on manufactures rather than materials and, more precisely, on manufactures expected or planned to have a long-term future within the United Kingdom, otherwise policy will forever sustain an increasingly anachronistic industrial base. This selectivity is not possible with devaluation and therefore an import control strategy looks even more attractive (other arguments are mustered by Ward, 1981), assuming that tariffs on manufactures work in the same way as would devaluation.

Whatever the precise accuracy of the above analysis, there is a strong general case for imposing controls over trade and capital flows in a world dominated by transnational corporations. As we have already argued, free trade and its related institutions, can increase the leverage of capital *vis-à-vis* both workers and the state in such a world. Conversely a willingness to intervene in trade and capital flows will tend to contain such leverage. An obviously ideal solution would be the creation of some powerful, supra-national institution for controlling transnationals. Interestingly, successive Conservative and Labour governments appear to have held the same view of the national interest in voting in favour of exempting the transnationals from close regulation (see Cable, 1980). This position will have to be fundamentally changed if democratic planning is to be successfully pursued. However, in the meantime, any attempt to plan trade will inevitably incur the wrath of exporting countries and various international institutions such as the EEC and GATT. The response of the Cambridge Economic Policy Group to this issue has been described as 'optimistic rationalism', and that of the TUC as 'cautious pragmatism' (Sharples, 1981). A more constructive response is required. If a country like Britain elects a government with a commitment to economic planning, then that government will have to make it clear that it is anxious to take part in new and urgent negotiations to establish a new international economic order in which a move to full employment at the level of the world economy is the urgent priority. The Brandt proposals may provide a convenient starting-point for such discussions.

Bottlenecks
Some have argued that the degree of excess capacity in the British economy (and in other economies) is less than the rate of unemployment so that capacity constraints, in terms of both capital and skills, can exist at relatively high levels of unemployment. Whilst it is clear that the long-term development of the British economy has been held back by the lack of investment in new technology and the development of human talent and skills, and that this has resulted in Britain's relatively high levels of unemployment, nevertheless it also seems clear that a much higher level of production could be achieved from existing capacity. As recently as 1979 more than one million additional people were employed than are employed today. What has happened since then to make their

re-employment impossible, given appropriate levels of demand? Some capacity has been scrapped but typically only the oldest machines and buildings. Much has been converted into smaller units, much is lying idle and, of course, excess capacity already existed to a substantial degree in 1979. Using the car industry as an example, relatively new plant is being used at nowhere near its capacity – the problem throughout Europe is excess capacity, not shortage. The components sector is still cutting back because of lack of demand. This is borne out by the Confederation of British Industry's *Industrial Trends Surveys* which have shown throughout the 1980s that a majority of respondents believed 'that lack of demand was likely to be an important factor in limiting output' with only small minorities believing that 'plant capacity would be an important factor'. The suggestion that capital stock is obsolescent has little operational significance in the short term for an economy with such an enormous level of unemployed people – there can surely be no doubt that putting more people to work using existing capacity would make a significant contribution to social welfare. If the obsolescence argument refers to the product, then it should be pointed out that there is currently much excess capacity for the latest products and models, and if the argument relates to the past increase in energy prices making capital equipment obsolescent, then this situation has changed dramatically.

The other potential bottlenecks which some observers have referred to is the availability of skilled manpower. Whilst this is indeed a problem in new industries employing new technology, reflecting the unwillingness of government and industry to get involved in adequate training programmes, the problem for short-run policies aiming at full employment can be overstated. Whilst excess demand for very specific skills in very specific locations is possible, throughout the 1980s the statistics reveal an extremely high rate of unemployed skilled craftsmen to unfilled vacancies. Should particular skills prove to be in short supply, then there are probably many people who would welcome a recall from early retirement.

Obviously all supply constraints on production and employment cannot be argued away. Any that remain must be identified and acted on immediately. There is plenty of capacity for training and for investment goods, and orders could be placed at an early stage by any administration following an expansionary strategy. It should also be remembered that the state still has direct control of steel and coal, together with much of the rest of the energy and transport sectors and an important element of the car industry, so that a commitment to expansion can immediately be translated into revised production and investment schedules in these sectors, therefore helping to minimise bottlenecks. Where bottlenecks remain, ways of using capacity more intensively, such as shift-working and weekend working, could be inaugurated. A more flexible approach to the use of capital capacity may also fit in with the part-time work requirements of much of the labour force, particularly women. At conventional full employment levels the British economy still contains much capacity which lies idle for a substantial proportion of the time, and also people who would welcome part-time employment if it were available.

Inflation
Whilst the issue of inflation is likely to loom larger as the economy approaches full employment, it is likely to appear as at least a political issue prior to that. With a commitment to return to full employment there will be an immediate effect on the environment within which prices and wages are determined. This, coupled with a depreciating or depreciated currency, could lead to some increase in the rate of inflation. However, the immediate dangers should not be over-dramatised and can be effectively countered in various ways. First of all, the economy is starting from a very low base and firms will be anxious to move output towards full capacity working rather than curtail it with substantial price increases, particularly as they are now, contrary to the popular view, operating generally with high mark-ups on marginal costs, representing a high degree of collusive behaviour induced by the adverse conditions of the slump (see Cowling, 1983). Interestingly, the stronger the commitment to sustained expansion, the lower will tend to be the rate of inflation *within* the transition period. If demand increases, but there is great uncertainty about whether or not it will persist, then firms will not respond with

an increase in output; but they will be induced to increase prices. As far as labour is concerned, it starts from a situation of an enormous excess supply which will continue to damp down wage demands; and this will probably be reinforced by its shattering experience of recent history.[16] This situation for both firms and workers, could be changed by the effects of a depreciating currency, although this could be countered by an appropriate cut in indirect taxes. The other point to recall is that the greater the reliance on the control of manufactured imports, the smaller the necessary depreciation consistent with the commitment to full employment as rapidly as possible. As argued earlier, there is every reason to expect that restricting the flow of imports of manufactures, by whatever means, will not have a significant impact on the price level, largely because the bulk of manufactured imports are not competitive in that sense, being controlled by transnational corporations with a domestic manufacturing base and a dominant position in the domestic market.

Thus inflationary problems are not expected to be significant in the short run. However, it is still desirable to institute mechanisms for inflation control within the transitional period so that experience is gained before the crunch period of full employment. A permanent system of price controls should be introduced as the basic structure of control over inflationary tendencies in a monopoly capitalist system.[17] Such controls would also negate any stagnationist tendencies arising from the growth of more concentrated structures in product markets, and would indeed remove one of the incentives for such growth. Whether or not wage controls are needed in addition to price controls is arguable. In a fully adjusted system workers would recognise a clear limit to wage bargaining imposed by the inflexibility of prices due to external control and would modify their behaviour accordingly. However, during the transitional period it is likely that lack of experience, confidence or information could lead to unanticipated bankruptcies and unemployment if there were no wage control system. It will also be desirable, as part of a system of democratic planning, to aim for a redistribution among labour as well as between labour and capital. The introduction of external wage controls would need to go hand in hand with the introduction of measures to secure economic democracy, which we shall discuss within the context of supply-side strategy in the next section.

SUPPLY-SIDE STRATEGY[18]

Complementary with a demand strategy aimed at a level of aggregate demand consistent with full employment, we need to articulate a supply-side strategy aimed at creating a democratic system of production and investment to replace that which is at present strategically controlled by the dominant transnational corporations. What we outline is a system in which democratic strategic planning takes a dominant role in the evolution of the industrial economy. The market will continue to play a substantial and crucial role, but it will work within the main long-term parameters set by government operating within a framework of broad-based democratic participation. We shall again use the extreme case of the United Kingdom to illustrate our proposals within a particular, concrete context. The case is extreme among the older industrialised countries in two senses – in terms of the depth of industrial crisis and also in terms of the absence of any sense of comprehensive industrial planning by the present administration. Nevertheless we see essentially the same response as being required among the generality of older industrial nations and, with inevitably different emphases, among a much wider array of countries, since, as we have already concluded, the fundamental economic issue facing the world is the erosion of national and regional economic autonomy by the dominant transnationals. For all countries in the capitalist world a more democratic system has to be counterposed to the present one, although the urgency of such a project will differ sharply from case to case.

THE POTENTIAL CONTRIBUTION OF DEMOCRATIC PLANNING

In a recent book on economic planning in Britain, Paul Hare

(1985) sees the main contribution of economic planning in terms of raising the volume of investment and improving its structure. He comes to this view on theoretical grounds – the market cannot be relied on to optimise the rate and direction of investment – and based on the observation of the poor growth performance of the British economy relative to that of the other advanced industrialised countries in the post-World War II period, which he ascribes to a combination of a relatively low level of investment coupled with a relatively low productivity of the investment which actually takes place. Thus the argument is about planning investment in general, since the theoretical argument applies in the case of any market economy, but also about the British case in particular. He points out that gross investment in Britain stagnated and fell in the 1970s and 1980s, with net investment showing the same sort of behaviour, but with a more dramatic fall post-1979. The share of investment in gross domestic product has been falling since 1970. Even more dramatically, net investment by industrial and commercial companies and by public corporations had fallen to virtually zero by 1982, and for manufacturing, construction and transport we have witnessed net *disinvestment* post-1979!

For Hare this sort of record justifies his concentration on the investment process and investment planning, and as long as we include within investment research and development and technical education and training, then we believe this emphasis is correct. However it does raise immediately the question, why was investment particularly low and particularly unproductive in Britain? Both could be explained by a lack of aggregate demand, and if so, one could just as well conclude that the concentration should be on raising demand rather than planning investment. We would simply point out that in general the two responses have to be considered as complementary: if more investment simply substitutes for consumption, then a higher level of investment will mean *more* unutilised capacity, which will in turn deter further investment. Whilst Hare clearly recognises the basic complementarity of expansionary macro-policies and economic planning, his concern for the level of investment leads him to the conclusion that the share of profits in gross domestic product has to be increased. Although having a superficial plausibility, we believe this conclusion to be misleading, both in terms of the funding of investment and the incentive to invest.

On the first point, the adequacy of the level of savings, Hare suggests that savings have been too low in Britain because of the history of the distribution of income between profits and wages, with falling profit share implying falling savings share. Therefore any government seeking to raise Britain's rate of investment must seek to increase the share of profits. In fact what we have observed over the post-war period is a tendency for the savings share of private income to increase quite rapidly. (We described this in the previous chapter.) It is therefore impossible to argue that the falling share of investment in Britain can be explained by a deficiency in domestic saving. Indeed, one can easily argue the opposite: the growth of involuntary saving (pension funds and corporate retentions) has served to hold back consumption and the adjustment in personal saving has failed to offset this effect: indeed it has contributed to it. Of course, the impact on aggregate demand could have been remedied by an increase in domestic investment, but this failed to occur. Instead it would appear that the funds available have been increasingly diverted to investment overseas. Over the period 1980–84, the outflow of total private sector savings amounted to more than £55 billion (see Johnson, 1985).

So what about the incentive to invest in Britain? In his discussion of the regulation of prices and wages, Hare concludes that underinvestment has arisen in Britain because of low profitability, and he therefore advocates that while wages should be controlled, prices should not. Thus a cut, or a lower growth rate, in real wages might be achieved which could contribute to raising the rate of investment. This needs analysing, both as an explanation of recent history and as a policy for the future.

The rate of profit (rate of return on capital) can be written down as the product of three components: the share of profits in gross domestic income; the rate of capacity utilisation, and the ratio of potential output to capital stock. Hare puts all the emphasis on the first component, which will of course be affected by the real wage; but it is clear that, for a given capital:potential output ratio, capacity utilisation is also relevant, and therefore the level of aggregate demand. It is also the case that capacity utilisation enters into the determination of the rate of profit via the profit share term, given the presence of overhead costs in addition to capital costs – the higher the level of capacity utilisation, the higher the share of profits. For the period identified by Hare as one of stagnation and decline in investment, the 1970s and 1980s (but particularly the period since 1979), there is much evidence of falling capacity utilisation, but little evidence of a fall in the price level relative to marginal cost (see Cowling, 1983). There is in fact some evidence that *extended* slump conditions tend to give rise to a higher degree of collusion within oligopoly groups resulting in *higher* mark-ups of price on marginal cost. Thus the period of the mid- to late 1970s and early 1980s has been largely a period characterised by high levels of excess capacity and a high level of prices relative to prime costs. Investment in the 1970s and 1980s would appear to have been retarded by low and declining levels of capacity utilisation, rather than by rising real wages (falling price-cost margins). This is supported by a whole range of empirical results showing that the single most important determinant of investment, in aggregate or at the industry level, is the rate of capacity utilisation, as argued in the previous chapter.

But what of the future? The observations above would suggest that the main hope for raising the level of investment would be via expansionary macroeconomic policies which would serve to increase capacity utilisation and thereby profitability. At full employment, profitability would be higher because of the capacity utilisation effect, but clearly any redistribution from profits to wages will tend to reduce the incentive to invest. Because of his concern with the volume of investment, Hare advocates distributional changes working in the opposite direction; changes which will typically be regressive. But this sort of position is only inevitable if other changes within the system are not considered. In any democratically planned economy the central theme is *society's* return on investment, and the division between profits and wages should not be of direct consequence for the level of investment. We need to think rather more about the institutional changes required when we no longer allow our concern with the volume of investment to dictate our stance on the distribution of income and wealth in our society. For example, if wages do take a larger share of the national cake, and yet we decide that the share of investment should increase, then we need institutions that can efficiently generate worker savings and channel them into domestic investment. Whilst the growth of pension funds has contributed to the growth of savings of workers, this may need supplementing with wage-earners' investment funds, as proposed in Sweden; particularly if wage share should increase significantly at full employment. A National Investment Bank, coupled to Sectoral, Regional and Local Enterprise Boards, could provide an appropriate channel for such funds, particularly if the state acts to guarantee the rate of return.

Whilst planning can make a contribution to raising the level of investment and improving its structure in any economy, since markets are typically not suited to handling long-term strategic matters, there are special reasons why planning can make a particularly significant contribution in the case of the British economy. Because British capital has such inter-national flexibility, as stressed in the previous chapter, it has a (relative) lack of long-term commitment to the British econ-omy as an arena of production and investment.[19] In the previous chapter we argued that this peculiarity of capital in Britain had led to the relatively poor performance of the British economy via the relatively low level of investment growth and, as a consequence, capacity utilisation was held down. This, in turn, served to depress still further the growth of investment. This is coupled with the peculiarly short-term perspective of British financial capital, linked to its history of primary involvement in funding trade and bond issues on a global basis, which, as a result, has meant that it has not been tied into a long-term domestic industrial perspective. To bend the system towards such a perspective will require changes in institutions, mechanisms and *people*. We must guard against simply installing within the new institutions the same sort of people who used to run the old.

But whilst all this is necessary, we have to arrange for its relative permanence. Since success on the supply side can only be achieved in the long term, we have to sustain the new system over the long term. There will be pressures in the short and medium term to reverse such changes and replace long-term with short-term perspectives; pressures *within* the government and civil service; pressures *on* the government and civil service from the City and industry (although possibly fractioned) and electoral pressure, in some cases orchestrated by the media. This leads to the fundamental requirement of broad-based *participation* in such a strategy. It will not succeed if imposed from the top – participative structures have to be at the core of planning. Indeed planning has to be seen as a way of extending our democracy into the economy (see Neuberger, 1985).

SOME PROPOSALS FOR INDUSTRIAL PLANNING IN BRITAIN

Paul Hare proposes a decentralised market-oriented planning system with the following features: a National Economic Planning Agency coordinating policy on investment, coupled with relatively autononous Sectoral, Regional and Local Agencies – without aiming to be comprehensive; together with democratically elected Planning Councils and a National Investment Bank. Implementation would be via voluntary agreement, but the regulation of incomes would be essential. Only temporary controls are seen as necessary over capital and trade flows, and the whole package would be seen as complementary with an expansionary macroeconomic policy (Hare, 1985).

Much of this we would support. It is very important to get away from any notion that comprehensive, centralised planning is either feasible or desirable. An appropriate strategy should seek to extend the role for planning within the economy whilst recognising an important and continuing role for markets. The author's emphasis on flexibility and his clear recognition that a complete set of planning institutions, or a complete coverage of industries at any particular conjuncture is not required, seem important points to make. His suggestions for a loose hierarchy of local, regional, sectoral and national plans, connected by information flows rather than instructions; experimenting with a variety of structures, but with the planning process as transparent as possible and with broad accountability to a series of planning councils with directly elected members, seem just right. His insistence that nationalisation is not an essential precondition for control, and may be a substitute for action on important issues, also seems valid. Where we would differ is in his specific package, which errs in favour of the French system rather than the Japanese, and in terms of the necessity for regulating the microeconomic environment within which the planning institutions operate. Before going into the details of our alternative package, we shall first raise what we regard as the central issues of economic democracy and the control of trade and capital flows.

He wants economic democracy to be limited because nothing should be allowed to interfere with the central objectives relating to the quantity and quality of investment, and he fears democracy may do damage to both: workers may choose to consume rather than save and, at the same time, they may want to restrict whatever savings they or the firm achieve to investment within their own enterprise. On the first point, whilst one can well imagine that, in a system without any participation on the part of workers in investment decisions there will generally be an unwillingness to defer consumption (and who is to say that it is not optimal?), this could be reversed by participation. On the second point, he seems a little unclear about his attitude to the usefulness of long-term commitment to a firm. On the one hand, he sees it as a positive virtue that Japanese firms and financial institutions make long-term commitments to the future of the enterprise, whilst he appears less enthusiastic about similar behaviour regarding investment on the part of workers. We need to examine this more closely.

The industrial regeneration of Britain requires a movement away from the guidelines of short-term profitability, but at the same time we have to safeguard ourselves from ossification. In other words, it will not in general be optimal to react to *short-term* market signals with sharp changes in long-term capital investment programmes, and thus the pressure of workers to secure the future of the firm may be appropriate, provided that the firm makes suitable adaptations. This can be achieved by emulating the behaviour of the typical, large, dominant corporation; but within a broader definition of the firm. Despite dramatic changes in the pattern of consumer expenditure, large, dominant firms demonstrate a remarkable propensity to persist and prosper; in many cases increasing their dominance. Entry to, and exit from, the top ranks of industry are rare. However, what is sustained, as we explained in earlier chapters, is the firm as a strategic decision-making entity, with its core of high-level management and technical expertise. The firm can persist in its dominant market position in advanced industrial countries, while production and investment may be largely relocated to low-wage, newly industrialising countries. Typically, such adaptation excludes from consideration most of the initial workforce. Economic democracy and social efficiency demand that adaptation to change requires a broader definition of the firm. The costs and benefits of change which are, at the moment, largely external to the firms' decision-making structure, have to be internalised. In Japan this is imperfectly achieved for part of the workforce by job security, but for those involved in subcontracting work for the giant Japanese corporations this is typically not available. Only much broader participation, by workers and by government, in strategic decision-making within the giant corporations will allow the emergence of patterns of growth and investment which are socially efficient. Pension funds and wage-earner investment funds plus equity holding by government could be used to help secure effective participation.

This provides a suitable point at which to examine Hare's view of the transnational corporation (and the control of trade and capital flows), since going transnational has been an important way of adapting to change. He argues that Britain's poor economic performance is unrelated to the role and power of these organisations and therefore economic planning need not include provisions for reducing such power. As we have argued earlier, we feel there is a strong, general, democratic case for imposing controls over trade and capital flows in a world of dominant transnational corporations. This is particularly the case in Britain. The difference in perspective would seem to arise as a consequence of a difference in view about which are the active and reactive agents within the economic system. His view (the orthodox view) is that the state sets the terms and the transnationals simply react passively. If profit rates are low in Britain then capital will move out – the government should thus act to secure better conditions for capital, rather than blaming the migration on capital. But, as we have argued throughout this book, these organisations are powerful enough to play a significant part in determining the framework within which the market operates. Labour force can be played off against labour force, and nation-state against nation-state, and the existence of relatively unified international markets provides an environment in which such leverage is at its maximum. It must also be true that even should transnationals react in a purely passive way to national governments, the national government should not simply accept the market's reaction. National government is there to reflect the democratic interest, and if that involves curtailing the ambitions of private economic organisations then that is what it should do. It is not obviously the case that, faced with capital flight, government should act to cut wages or taxes on capital, rather than seek to curtail flight by more direct action. We now turn to the details of our industrial strategy which are based on such action.

We have already examined our demand-side strategy and can accept that an expansionary macroeconomic stance will be the most important element in achieving a short-term turnaround in industrial performance. But Keynesianism, whilst having a centrally important role in moving the economy back to full employment and full capacity working via fiscal and monetary expansion, is inevitably limited in its effect. It deals with symptoms rather than underlying causes. The underlying causes of Britain's poor record of productivity growth will not have been addressed, so that the tendency to relative decline will not have been reversed, except that industry operating in a more conducive environment provided by the expansion in demand would tend to raise its level of investment and would also experience a higher productivity of the investment undertaken. Expansionary demand-side policies must be complemented with a supply-side strategy aimed

at rectifying those deficiencies of the British industrial economy which lie at the root of Britain's relatively poor economic
performance. The short-run Keynesian policies of a redirected
Treasury must be coupled with a commitment to an aggressive
and expansionary supply-side strategy, formulated and imple-
mented by a newly constituted, high-powered and relatively
autonomous Industry Department working through a highly
decentralised structure.

What of the form of planning? We feel that an adaptation
of the Japanese model would be most effective. Whilst the
French approach to planning has been relatively passive (at
least prior to and since the 1981 socialist government), largely
directed at providing coordination and information flows
between sectors, and thus promoting efficiency, the Japanese
approach has been much more aggressive, and aimed at
reshaping the industrial landscape by strategic and selective
interventions: the Japanese government has a direct and
intimate involvement in 'strategic industries' (see Johnson,
1982). It is not simply involved in creating a suitable environment for industry, but intervening directly in decision-making.
Japan is the most successful example of a country, late to
industrialise, requiring the government itself to lead the drive
to industrialise, and again requiring such a lead in the trauma
of military defeat. Although much less dramatic, Britain is in a
similar position today as a relatively undeveloped member of
the group of advanced industrial countries. The dominance of
the regulatory function of government has to be displaced by
its developmental function – that is, its direct involvement in
the birth, growth and death of industries. But in neither
strategic planning of the future, nor allocative procedures of
the present, should the system be a pure one. Industrial policy
will partially supplant the market system, but the market will
continue through the interstices of such strategic planning –
the democratic strategy would incorporate the market. This is
where we have to distinguish our strategy from that of the
Japanese. In the latter case industrial policy appears as a
reflection of economic nationalism, where nationalistic policies are aimed essentially at supporting the interests of national capital. In the case of democratic planning, industrial
policy appears as an attempt by national, regional and local

communities to regain control of their economic futures. The general approach to planning will be similar, but the detailed structures and the ultimate objectives will be very different.

Industries, both old and new, which appear viable and indeed strategically important in a long-run perspective, but which are vulnerable in the short or medium term without significant intervention, have to be identified. Such industries have to be provided with the resources, commitment and protection to allow them to grow and mature, so that in the longer term the degree of intervention can be progressively reduced. The infant industry argument for protection and intervention has a significance in advanced industrial economies as well as developing economies, and has a particular significance in post-Thatcher Britain, where manufacturing industry especially has been so ravaged over such a short time-interval (see Hare, 1985).

However, it is clear that such intervention is a difficult and dangerous project. It is difficult to identify certain areas of economic activity on which resources should be concentrated, and, as a result, tend to neglect others; and it is also potentially dangerous to protect certain areas of economic activity from the discipline of international competition. Nevertheless, given the urgency of the task and given the resources available, we have to face up to the consequences of selective intervention and, as we have already argued, it is *not* the case that free trade imposes a beneficial discipline in a world of dominant, transnational corporations.

We have raised earlier the relevance of the Japanese approach to planning, but the preconditions for successful planning in Britain are very different from what they were in Japan when MITI (the Ministry of International Trade and Industry) intervened so successfully in the making of Japan's economic future. We need to identify clearly that part of the Japanese experience which could be transplanted to Britain, but also that part which could not. We suspect that what is needed is something like MITI plus a variety of participative structures aimed at generating a broad consensus in favour of such intervention. This may appear paradoxical. It is often claimed that MITI's success can be partly attributed to a lack of democracy − a coherent civil service/business community untrammelled by the dictates of democracy was able to engineer a successful joint strategy for the sectors targeted, and the strategy was allowed to develop over the long term without being undermined by electoral change. But it is obvious that the culture, society, history and politics of Japan are very different from those of Britain. The democratic argument has to be inverted. *Because* no broad consensus for economic planning exists in Britain it has to be created, and it can only be created by involving people in the process itself. This suggests first that participation is essential for the success of our industrial strategy (and it can be achieved at various levels and in various forms and, of course, applies also to Japan), and second that a piecemeal/step-by-step approach is required to allow people to get used to it. How would we begin this step-by-step process? As mentioned earlier, we should start with those sectors of the economy in which the government already has substantial control and in which there is a general recognition that a lack of planning has been an impediment to performance in the past. Energy and transport would be obvious candidates (see Hare, 1985), and a commitment to careful, realistic planning in these sectors could provide an important platform for transforming the way in which economic problems are approached in Britain. It is glaringly obvious to a broad spectrum of the people of Britain that strategies for coal, oil, electricity and gas need to be coordinated for any sensible pattern of energy production and use to emerge; similarly with rail and road transport. We already have a broad consensus for such policies. The spill-over from the successful planning of these sectors would be a growing willingness to accept that economic planning has a crucial role within a market economy.

We would also need to make an immediate strategic commitment to other key sectors, either because it is essential that increased capacity be secured for the general expansion in demand, or because of the precarious nature of certain key industries, with the British car industry being a centrally important example. A slightly more relaxed view can be taken of other, potentially important, relatively *new* industries which require long-term funding by the state. We suspect that the sort of industry to target in the immediate future is the one where there is heavy state involvement already in terms of the infrastructure and manpower, but where there is no follow-through in terms of intervention and support within the industrial organisation of production and marketing. We believe there are important cases where the development of such industries is being held back by the absence of such intervention and where, if such intervention did take place it would be widely regarded as the next logical step, given the already heavy involvement of public money, and also appropriate, given the rather limited development prospects at present. Some industries which may fall in this category are biotechnology, computer software and fashion. In each case there is a heavy public involvement via university biology and computer science and the art colleges, and yet it is doubtful whether this has led to national economic success because of the siphoning-off of such talent by giant international companies. Without a *national* strategy our future in these important and growing areas will largely be taken out of our hands. The central point is that when the market economy is failing the national economy, intervention should not stop at the level of education and training, but should extend to industrial organisation and strategy as well. Opportunities need to be created within Britain where such talent can find fulfilment *and* contribute to national economic success.

This is an appropriate point to consider briefly the planning of our scientific activity. There has to be a fundamental reorganisation of government-funded research and development. Associated with the peculiarly international perspective of British capital, the British state has retained the ambition of remaining a global power which has in turn led to the present budget allocating most resources to military/aerospace R & D, which has had a very limited economic pay-off for the domestic productive economy. This money has to be reallocated to research on manufacturing production and new product development over a broad range of industries. However, we have to recognise that our ability to make scientific advances in the short and medium term is determined largely by the current stock of qualified scientists and engineers. Given this, we have to think of how the desired reallocation can be achieved. We do not believe the market can easily handle this. Unless congenial and challenging opportunities are available elsewhere in the national economy, displacing scientists from employment on military/aerospace R & D will simply increase the rate of outmigration from Britain to the United States. It is unlikely that much of manufacturing is capable of responding. They are unscientific because of the absence of scientists, and because of the absence of scientists they do not see the need for more. Even if they do, they will in most cases not be able to use them effectively. We could seek to break out from vicious to virtuous circle by giving an enhanced role to the universities. Collaborative projects between industry and universities could be encouraged and funded, and these would supply exciting and challenging jobs for scientists released from other areas of activity.

In the above discussion we have opted for economic planning along the lines of the Japanese approach of selective intervention; but just as the Japanese were clear about the *national* basis of industrial expansion, we must be clear that a successful industrial strategy implies that we commit ourselves to establishing a considerable degree of control over the dominant transnational corporations operating in Britain, whether of *domestic* or *foreign* origin. We have already argued that a cause of Britain's relative industrial decline during the twentieth century is the relatively high degree of internationalisation of British capital. Most recently it seems that the rapid deindustrialisation of Britain can be linked to the activities of the transnationals. (See our analysis of the evidence in the previous chapter.) Whatever the precise reasons for such changes, they will remain relatively irreversible without direct intervention. Undoubtedly, setting the British economy on a sustained expansionary path will encourage these firms to greater investment in Britain, but it will not be a sufficient condition; and in the meantime the expansion itself will be jeopardised by the consequences of the past decisions of the transnationals in terms of the high potential propensity of the British economy to import in the future as expansion takes place.

Control over the transnationals has to be established, but equally clearly, this is an objective not easily realised. Realistic, but inevitably limited, measures which can be taken in the short term can grow out of local, regional, national and European initiatives. Thus Enterprise Boards at local and regional level can seek to gain influence within British-based transnationals. Closely associated with this, trustees on Pension Fund boards can seek to establish some sort of control over the flow of funds, and ensure that Enterprise Board initiatives are funded and that overseas investment is subject to close scrutiny. Such activity could obviously be greatly helped by fiscal changes promoting domestic rather than foreign investment. At the national level the regulation of capital and trade flows will be required to ensure the phased expansion of the British economy. Whilst an international approach to the regulation of the transnationals is obviously desirable, it is important not to be pessimistic about what can be achieved at the national level. The nation-state, *if it chooses to use it*, has substantial leverage. For example, to return to the case of the 'British' car industry, it is clear that the government could achieve much in terms of the expansion of production and investment in the United Kingdom by the American transnationals if it were willing to threaten them with progressive exclusion from the profitable UK market for cars – prices within the United Kingdom are still very much higher than in the rest of Europe. Clearly, there are enormous political difficulties, not least the regulations of the EEC, but a determination to intervene decisively in a particularly crucial sector would provide a salutary lesson for the transnationals in general. However, as well as acting independently, Britain should reverse its present stance regarding the international control of the transnationals. It is clear that a voluntary code of conduct for the transnationals is insufficient. Such a code may appear under the guise of international control *over* the transnationals, but it is better seen as a code of conduct *amongst* the transnationals themselves (Fine, 1983). Whilst a more effective policy may be sought within the United Nations, perhaps a more immediately effective policy could be campaigned for within Europe, and specifically within the EEC. General concern about deindustrialisation could be used as a platform from which to advance a policy for effectively regulating the production and investment policies of the transnationals, at least within Europe, and hopefully growing into a more global strategy allowing the EEC to take a much more positive role in development issues.

NEW INSTITUTIONS

Whilst institutions with a strategic planning role are a necessary part of any attempt to introduce a long-term perspective to economic policy-making in Britain, the institutions themselves are derivative from a prior commitment to such a fundamental change in policy. They therefore represent a commitment to replace the short-term perspective of the Treasury view, and that of the financial institutions, with one much more favourable to industry and to production. Coupled with this has to be a commitment to intervene decisively in the strategies of the transnationals and to act to secure a democratic structure of intervention and development. Without such commitments, as we have already argued, no matter what the new structure of institutions, such policy will founder on short-term expedients, the conservatism of the civil service, the power of the transnationals, or the resistance of the people. Of central importance is the establishment of the case for decisive intervention in industry to secure a long-term reversal in its relative (or absolute) decline. Institutions can formalise the commitment to such policies, and their structure, procedures and personnel can act to ensure that such commitments cannot easily be reversed; but they are simply ratifying some position already established. The history of planning in Britain shows how fragile was the commitment, despite the creation of many new institutions. The lack of teeth of the Department of Economic Affairs was obvious and could be said to be due to the Treasury view predominating. But, more recently, we have seen how the Treasury view is malleable. With clear goals, and a determination to pursue them, institutions with teeth should be forthcoming.

A revamped and reorganised Department of Trade and Industry (DTI), of equal status to the Treasury, is needed – a power-house dedicated to raising the quantity and quality of investment in British industry. Economic policy will be organised around the twin pillars of Treasury and Industry; the former with a short-term demand perspective, the latter with a longer-term supply perspective. The new DTI will be organised around the requirements of a Strategic Planning Agency, with a long-term commitment of substantial funds and the powers to intervene decisively in crucial sectors of the economy in terms of both long-term funding and controlling trade and capital movements. A separate state holding company might be useful to manage any equity involvement the government may acquire in the evolution of its industrial strategy and could indeed have a creative role in the development of new enterprises. Fused with the DTI would be a National Investment Bank (NIB) to ensure that industrial strategy and associated financial arrangements are closely integrated. The Bank would provide a suitable agency for raising additional funds for long-term investment from pension funds and the money market, and could provide appropriate guarantees.

But planning would be neither comprehensive nor centralised. A loose hierarchy linking the DTI and NIB with other government departments involved in industrial investment (e.g. Energy and Transport) and with Sectoral Agencies and Regional and Local Enterprise Boards would decentralise much of the work of the department. The DTI would remain as the central coordinating agency but it would lie at the apex of an information structure, not a command structure. Variety and flexibility would be the essence of the planning structure and there would be no necessary attempt to cover all sectors, nor all regions, of the economy. The areas of activity covered would reflect the priorities established at the centre and within the regions.

Alongside the agencies themselves would be elected Industry or Planning Councils to which the agencies would submit their plans for discussion and approval. It would also be a requirement of any firm receiving funds that approved participative structures within the enterprise be established. By these means the involvement of people within the system of industrial intervention will be gradually expanded and will serve to secure the future of such intervention.

Control over the transnationals, along the lines previously described, will be sought at national level via the DTI, but also at other levels, with information flows up and down the hierarchy serving to help coordinate such control. There remains the question of the control of monopoly power. Policies to protect and support the growth of domestic industry may provide fertile ground for the creation and exercise of monopoly power. Whilst in Japan domestic competition appeared to flourish in those industries protected from foreign competition, we cannot easily assume the same thing will automatically happen in Britain. Active intervention in specific industries to secure rapid development should be accompanied by regulatory measures to contain the exercise of monopoly power and ensure that the entry into the industry of new firms is not held back by dominant extant corporations. Indeed we shall need an active strategy to support the birth and development of new firms, including workers' cooperatives and management buy-outs.

A NEW WORLD ORDER

We have mapped out a system of democratic planning to counterpose to the existing system dominated by the transnationals. But we have done it only within a specific national context. We need now to see how such a system might be generalised. Do the suggestions made for Britain have any substantial validity in the case of other nation-states, and how might an international system work when made up of nation states each anxious to pursue democratic national strategies? We turn first to the question of whether exploring the British case offers any general guidelines.

By taking Britain as our example we inevitably focus attention on the development of a democratic alternative to the dominance of the transnationals in the context of the structure and institutions of the older advanced industrial countries. Thus we are establishing a structure of intervention which might have relevance within Europe and the United States,[20] with appropriate recognition of the many differences between such economies, but may appear to have only limited relevance to either the underdeveloped or newly-industrialising parts of the world. Obviously there is some truth in this.

We are saying little about the unique features of the underdeveloped or newly-industrialising parts of the world. Nevertheless, we have tried to raise the issue of the general system effect of the transnationals at the level of the world economy – a neo-imperialism of free trade where such an imperialism is that of the transnationals. Thus what we have to say about an alternative system is counterposed to that new imperialism, and therefore, to that extent, is generalisable. The alternative offered is a system of national democratic planning comprising both demand-side and supply-side elements which we see as necessary in establishing full democracies in all nation states. The management of aggregate demand to ensure full employment is both an inevitable demand of democracy and a crucial ingredient in sustaining the forces of democracy otherwise held back by the forces of the new imperialism.[21] On the supply side we view it as essential that democratic control is gained over production and investment in a world where planning is otherwise done by transnational capital with a private, yet global, perspective.[22] Inevitable inconsistencies between the objectives of capital and the national community provide the requirement for national industrial planning in advanced, underdeveloped and newly industrialising countries. Whilst the policies of the transnationals may appear to be favouring the newly industrialising nations, there can be no presumption that the process and form of industrialisation is compatible with the long-term ambitions of such communities. The Japanese case of relatively autonomous national economic development is an important example of what can be achieved outside the main capitalist orbit. The fact that it was still capitalism should not detract from the significance of the case. The approach remains valid within the context of democratic economic planning.[23]

The second question we turn to is the nature of the new world system of relatively autonomous national economies implied by the strategies we advocate.[24] At first sight this may appear as a paradoxical response to the imperialism of the transnationals. A more conventional response is to accept the existing order and then, in some cases, to recognise national Keynesianism as increasingly anachronistic in such a world. The logic of this position then demands a coordinated response across nations to secure a break-out from world stagnation. Thus supra-national institutions are seen to be the appropriate response to an integrated international economy in crisis. However, whilst recognising that a coordinated reflation of the world economy could form an important component of any viable response to world stagnation, it should be seen as the culmination of a process in which a network of relatively autonomous national communities is created, rather than simply representing the injection of a higher level of demand into a world economic system which otherwise remains fundamentally unchanged, with all its inevitable contradictions. We wish to counterpose a network of viable autonomous communities to a spurious internationalism.

We are seeking an internationalism in the true sense of such aspirations – one of peace and harmony, preserving and enhancing a variety of cultures rather than leading to the swamping of culture and community in a homogeneous and amorphous world created by the dominant corporations acting as the agents of the dominant culture which they themselves have played a central part in forming. Without active, democratic intervention in the economic forces swirling round the world economy, the outcome will inevitably be the continued suppression of minority cultures whenever they remain without the backing of the dominant agents of the economic system. A managed cultural convergence is a predictable consequence of the present system. In contrast, heterogeneous, polycentric developments will be allowed within a system emphasising national economic autonomy. Establishing such a system, and also extending it to regional and local level, is at the core of our proposals. And yet, were one to take the media as representing the popular view, we are clearly advancing unpopular demands. One could easily come to the same view with respect to economists. We are awash in a sea of comment which unreservedly recommends the free play of market forces at the international level; protectionism is bad, opening up markets is good. This is not simply a view advanced by the Right, alongside most of the important supra-national economic institutions which now also tend to represent the views of the Right – institutions such as the

International Monetary Fund, the World Bank, GATT, OECD[25] – but also by most Keynesian and liberal commentators.[26] To our mind, simplistic economic arguments which once had substantial validity, and which of course retain some validity, are being pushed far too far by otherwise reasonable people, to the exclusion of other far more fundamental matters which relate to the character of our culture.[27] The flowering of a multiplicity of cultures requires barriers to international forces: barriers not to people and ideas, but to capital. We need to nurture the roots of our society by establishing the autonomy of small communities but, paradoxically, in a monopoly capitalist world, this requires state intervention to secure a level of aggregate demand consistent with full employment plus a strategic commitment to national industrial development.

Many will see any attempt to cut off the nation-state from some of the forces of the international economy as beggar-my-neighbour policies. In a world stagnating under such forces this would seem wide of the mark. The aim of such a strategy is not to induce a stagnation of demand for the output of the rest of the system, but to establish the conditions whereby a particular society can thrive and prosper. We have argued that to achieve this at the current historical juncture requires that individual nations sever at least some of the international connections which have been established by transnational capital. The consequences of such action we foresee as a rapid movement to full employment and to a growth path with a historically high gradient, together with a more equitable distribution of income and wealth. Dynamic, fully employed economies are not a threat to each other, but they cannot be established without some degree of isolation from world capitalist forces. Such isolation will ensure not only the revived development of the older industrial economies, but also the full and balanced development of the underdeveloped and newly industrialising countries. The new world order will be polycentric rather than hierarchical; democratic rather than authoritarian; and will allow for the growth of a true internationalism out of a firm base of national autonomy.

NOTES

1. The early sections of this chapter are adapted from Cowling (1985).
2. At the time this is being written the extreme case of South Africa is the centre of attention. The pressure of the disenfranchised has clearly changed the position of the dominant economic interests regarding political democracy but they have yet to convince the dominant Afrikaans political interests.
3. Does this denial extend to intervention by the state in terms of the strategic planning of the enterprise? This will be determined by the purpose of such intervention. If the State is simply acting as an executive committee for capital, then its role will in general not be denied by capital. However, if its role is to establish democratic control over the enterprise then the nature of capitalism will be fundamentally changed.
4. Jacquemin and de Jong (1977) survey the relevant estimates for Europe and the United States.
5. Cohen (1981), pp. 307–8, has defined 'First Rank' and 'Second Rank' global headquarters cities. New York, Tokyo and London comprise the former group, with Osaka, Rhine-Ruhr, Chicago, Paris, Frankfurt and Zurich the second.
6. The cultural poverty of recent developments in our provincial cities reflects such changes. Nineteenth-century Manchester, Liverpool and Birmingham benefited substantially from the fact that local industry was locally based. As control of the major corporations with production units in these cities has moved away, so has the provision of funding for major cultural initiatives. Undoubtedly local authorities have tried to fill the gap, but they have been severely handicapped by these deeper processes. However, we suspect also that the global headquarters cities are not really gaining. The few who control the major transnational corporations no longer have close connections or affinities with the people of any city and as a result even the key cities of the world like London and New York may be receiving less broad cultural investment from private benefactions.
7. We have already suggested that such policy changes result partly from the pressure of business for policies consistent with labour discipline. We have also argued that the existence of the transnational organisation of production will also work in the same direction given that excessive wage demands will more likely get translated into job losses.
8. It will be argued that international policy coordination offers a way out. Certainly an international reflation will pose fewer problems than Keynesianism in one country. But, in addition to all the inevitable problems of coordination, there remains the basic stumbling-block of monopoly capitalism not being easily operable at full employment because of the dynamic consequences for the balance of power between capital and labour. The technical solution of international policy coordination by no means guarantees those policies to be full employ-

ment ones. For that, deeper political and economic changes will be required.

9. We are, of course, assuming that crowding out is not an important phenomenon at this time. We agree with Currie (1981) that crowding out has more to do with restrictive monetary policy than expansionary fiscal policy, since accommodating monetary policy is always possible. The precise form of fiscal and monetary policy will not be discussed here, but obviously a combination which alleviated the potential problems associated with a return to full employment would be favoured. For example if, as is indeed the case, there is a substantial excess capacity in the building industry, then rapid expansion of public expenditure on housing would seem a suitable component of fiscal expansion. Such expenditure would probably also minimise leakage via imports, and thus contribute to the alleviation of a further potential problem.

10. The difficulty remains, however, as we have emphasised earlier, that the output response will be observed within a different polity. Thus the Keynesian policies adopted by one country may have only a limited impact within that polity, although having a full impact globally. Thus transnationalism imposes a disincentive to the *national* adoption of Keynesian policies.

11. This could, of course, also be achieved by measures to secure a rapid increase in *public* employment where the decisions are made directly by the state.

12. The existence of incremental employment subsidies would reduce the attraction of overtime working from the demand side, which would probably mean a decline in the length of the working week.

13. Some would argue that technological progress means that job growth will be less than this, but this will tend to be counterbalanced by the fact that much of the initial employment impact will be in public sector, labour-intensive, production. The multiplier effects from this initial injection of expenditure will then work through the whole system and in combination with the initial impact on employment may suggest a total effect similar to our rough calculations.

14. Britain's membership of the EEC of course raises real problems. In the short term, expedients such as informal import controls, non-tariff barriers and temporary controls can be utilised. In the longer term, EEC regulations on the activities of the transnationals are required. This will be pursued later in the chapter.

15. A fuller theoretical analysis, coupled with some empirical investigation of pricing in the European car market, is contained in Cowling and Sugden (1986).

16. Recently there has been much discussion of the high rate of real wage growth in Britain, despite the high level of unemployment. However, what is clear is the substantial disparity between the experience of manual and non-manual workers in the slump of the 1980s. Real wage growth for manual workers had been minimal, whilst those within the

managerial and technical hierarchy have experienced a substantial growth in their salaries (see Dowrick, 1986).

17. The system of flexible, but permanent, price controls proposed in Bowles, Gordon and Weisskopf (1984) and based on tax disincentives rather than administrative regulation would appear to have some attractive properties. They reject wage controls on the grounds that inflation is primarily due to the stagnation of productivity growth and the appropriate response is therefore to do something about that, rather than simply focusing on wages. We have a lot of sympathy for such an approach.

18. This section is adapted from Cowling (1987).

19. In a world of dominant transnational corporations, as we have argued before, this is a *general* phenomenon. We are simply arguing that the British case is, again, an extreme one.

20. Interesting suggestions for a democratic alternative in the United States have been made by Bluestone and Harrison (1982) and by Bowles *et al.* (1984).

21. Some may argue that the world is divided into a demand-constrained part (the North) and a supply-constrained part (the South). Whilst we see an element of truth in this we would wish to argue that in each part the efficient expansion of output requires intervention in terms of both demand and supply. Given the stagnation of the 1970s and 1980s, the South contains massive amounts of unutilised capacity, whilst in the North it is insufficient simply to adopt Keynesian policies.

22. The *Brandt Report* (1980), whilst arguing for a greatly increased investment by the North in the South, fails to demand a fundamental change in the institutions and mechanisms of development. Recommendations are made for some regulation of the activity of the transnationals, but it again looks like regulation *among* them, rather than *over* them. The requirements of the democratic control of development by relatively autonomous countries, or groups of countries, are not really addressed.

23. It may, of course, be the case that small national economies will find it necessary to band together in order to achieve a higher degree of group economic autonomy. This will probably require joint demand and industrial strategies in addition to customs unions.

24. Hymer (1972) developed a vision of such a world, but did not get into the detail of the nature of national planning.

25. The honourable exceptions are the various agencies of the United Nations.

26. Whilst writing this, one of the authors received a newsletter from the British Fulbright Scholars Association in which Senator Fulbright himself points out that study in another country is likely to lead to 'some appreciation of the essential futility of nationalistic economic policies and of the way in which an international division of labour benefits all countries'.

27. Keynes himself was dubious of the net benefits of the international

division of labour and advocated a substantial degree of self-sufficiency and economic isolation because 'we all need to be as free as possible of interference from economic changes elsewhere, in order to make our own favourite experiments towards the ideal social republic of the future'. (See Keynes (1982), p.241.)

References

Aaronovitch, S. and R. Smith (1981), *The Political Economy of British Capitalism: A Marxist Analysis*, London, McGraw-Hill.

Ádám, Gyorgy (1975), 'Multinational Corporations and Worldwide Sourcing', in Hugo Radice (ed.), *International Firms and Modern Imperialism*, London, Penguin.

Andrews, Kenneth R. (1980), *The Concept of Corporate Strategy*, Homewood, Richard D. Irwin.

Baran, Paul A. and Paul M. Sweezy (1966), *Monopoly Capital*, Harmondsworth, Penguin.

Barnet, Richard J. and Ronald E. Müller (1974), *Global Reach*, New York, Simon and Schuster.

Benson, I. and J. Lloyd (1983), *New Technology and Industrial Change*, London, Kogan Page.

Berg, S. A. (1986), 'Excess Capacity and the Degree of Collusion: The Norwegian Experience 1967–82', *International Journal of Industrial Organization*, 4.

Berle, Adolf A. and Gardiner C. Means (1932), *The Modern Corporation and Private Property*, New York, Macmillan.

Berthomieu, C. and A. Hanaut (1980), 'Can International Subcontracting Promote Industrialisation?', *International Labour Review*, 119.

Bhaduri, A. and J. Steindl (1983), 'The Rise of Monetarism as a Social Doctrine', *Thames Papers in Political Economy*.

Blanchflower, David (1984), 'Comparative Pay Levels in Domestically-Owned Manufacturing Plants: A Comment', *British Journal of Industrial Relations*, 22.

Bluestone, B. and B. Harrison (1982), *The Deindustrialization of America*, New York, Basic Books.

Bowles S., D. Gordon and T. Weisskopf (1984), *Beyond the Wasteland: A Democratic Alternative to Economic Decline*, New York, Anchor Press.

Boyer, Marcel and Michel Moreaux (1983), 'Conjectures, Rationality and Duopoly Theory', *International Journal of Industrial Organization*, 1.

Brandt Report (1980), *North South: A Programme for Survival*, London, Pan Books.

Bresnahan, Timothy (1981), 'Duopoly Models with Consistent Conjectures', *American Economic Review*, 71.

Brown, Wilson B. (1984), 'Firm-like Behaviour in Markets: The Administered Channel', *International Journal of Industrial Organization*, 2.

Buckley, Peter J. (1981), 'A Critical Review of Theories of the Multinational Enterprise', *Aussenwirtschaft*, 36.

Buckley, Peter J. and Mark Casson (1976), *The Future of the Multinational Enterprise*, London, Macmillan.

Buckley, Peter J. and Peter Enderwick (1983), 'Comparative Pay Levels in Domestically-Owned and Foreign-Owned Plants in UK Manufacturing: Evidence from the 1980 Workplace Industrial Relations Survey', *British Journal of Industrial Relations*, 21.

Bulow, Jeremy I., John D. Geanakoplos and Paul D. Klemperer (1985), 'Multimarket Oligopoly: Strategic Substitutes and Complements', *Journal of Political Economy*, 93.

Burkitt, Brian (1982), 'Collective Bargaining, Inflation and Incomes Policy', in D. Currie and M. Sawyer (eds), *Socialist Economic Review*, London, Merlin.

Burkitt, Brian and David Bowers (1979), *Trade Unions and the Economy*, London, Macmillan.

Burman, J. P. (1970), 'Capacity Utilisation and the Determinants of Fixed Investment', in K. Holton and D. F. Heathfield (eds), *The Econometric Study of the UK*, London, Macmillan.

Cable, V. (1980), *British Interests and Third World Development*, London, Overseas Development Institute.

Casson, Mark (1980), 'The Theory of Foreign Direct Investment', *University of Reading Discussion Papers in International Investment and Business Studies*, No. 50.

Caves, Richard E. (1971), 'International Corporations: the Industrial Economics of Foreign Investment', *Economica*, 38.

Caves, Richard E. (1982), *Multinational Enterprise and Economic Analysis*, Cambridge, Cambridge University Press.

Chandler, Alfred D. (1962), *Strategy and Structure*, Cambridge, Mass., MIT Press.

Channon, Derek F. (1979), *Multinational Strategic Planning*, London, Macmillan.

CIS (1978), *Anti-report: the Ford Motor Company*, Anti-report No. 20, Counter Information Services.

Clarke, Roger (1982), 'Oligopoly and Myopic Behaviour', *Journal of Economic Studies*, 9.

Clarke, Roger and Stephen W. Davies (1982), 'Market Structure and Price-Cost Margins', *Economica*, 49.

Coase, Ronald H. (1937), 'The Nature of the Firm', *Economica*, 4.

Cohen, R. B. (1981), 'The New International Division of Labour, Multinational Corporations and Urban Hierarchy', in M. Dear and A. J. Scott (eds), *Urbanisation and Urban Planning in Capitalist Society*, London, Methuen.

Cowling, Keith (1981), 'Oligopoly, Distribution and the Rate of Profit', *European Economic Review*, 15.

Cowling, Keith (1982), *Monopoly Capitalism*, London, Macmillan.

Cowling, Keith (1983), 'Excess Capacity and the Degree of Collusion: Oligopoly Behaviour in the Slump', *Manchester School*, LI.

Cowling, Keith (1985), 'Economic Obstacles to Democracy', in R.C.O. Matthews, *Economy and Democracy*, London, Macmillan.

Cowling, Keith (1986), 'The Internationalisation of Production and Deindustrialisation', in A. Amin and J. Goddard (eds), *Technological Change, Industrial Restructuring and Regional Development*, London, Allen and Unwin.

Cowling, Keith (1987), 'An Industrial Strategy for Britain: the Nature and Role of Planning', *International Journal of Applied Economics*, 1.

Cowling, Keith and Michael Waterson (1976), 'Price Cost Margins and Market Structure', *Economica*, 43.

Cowling, Keith and Ian Molho (1982), 'Wage Share, Concentration and Unionism', *Manchester School*, L.

Cowling, Keith and Roger Sugden (1986), 'Exchange Rate Adjustment and Oligopoly Pricing Behaviour', Mimeo, March.

Craypo, Charles (1975), 'Collective Bargaining in the Conglomerate, Multinational Firm: Litton's Shutdown of Royal Typewriter', *Industrial and Labour Relations Review*, 29.

Cubbin, John and Dennis Leech (1983), 'The Effects of Shareholding Dispersion on the Degree of Control in British Companies', *Economic Journal*, 93.

Currie, David (1981), 'What's Left of Monetarism?', in David Currie and Ron Smith (eds), *Socialist Economic Review*, London, Merlin.

Currie, David and R. P. Smith (1981), 'Economic Trends and the Crisis in the UK Economy', *Socialist Economic Review*, London, Merlin.

Cyert, R. M. and J. G. March (1963), *A Behavioral Theory of the Firm*, Englewood Cliffs, Prentice-Hall.

Dicken, Peter (1986), *Global Shift*, London, Harper and Row.

Dixit, Avinash and Nick Stern (1982), 'Oligopoly and Welfare: a Unified Presentation with Applications to Trade and Development', *European Economic Review*, 19.

Donsimoni, Marie-Paul, Paul Geroski and Alexis Jacquemin (1984), 'Concentration Indices and Market Power: Two Views', *Journal of Industrial Economics*, 32.

Dowrick, S. (1983), 'Notes on Transnationals', Mimeo, Department of Economics, University of Warwick.

Dowrick, S. (1986), 'Bargaining over Surplus: Oligopolies, Workers and the Distribution of Income', PhD Thesis, University of Warwick.

Drucker, Peter (1961), *The Practice of Management*, London, Mercury.

Dunning, John H. (1976), *United States Industry in Britain*, London, Wilton House Publications.

Dunning, John H. (1977), 'Trade, Location of Economic Activity and the Multinational Enterprise: a Search for an Eclectic Approach', in Bertil Ohlin, Per-Ove Hesselborn and Per Magnus Wijkman (eds), *The International Allocation of Economic Activity*, London, Macmillan.

Dunning, John H. (1979), 'Explaining Changing Patterns of International Production: in Defence of the Eclectic Theory', *Oxford Bulletin of Economics and Statistics*, 41.

Dunning, John H. (1980), 'Toward an Eclectic Theory of International Production: Some Empirical Tests', *Journal of International Business Studies*, 11.

Dunning, John H. (1981), 'Explaining the International Direct Investment Position of Countries: Towards a Dynamic or Developmental Approach', *Weltwirtschaftliches Archiv*, 117.

Dunning, John H. (ed.) (1985), *Multinational Enterprises, Economic Structure and International Competitiveness*, Chichester, Wiley.

Dunning, John H. and Eleanor J. Morgan (1980), 'Employee Compensation in US Multinationals and Indigenous Firms: an Exploratory Micro/Macro Analysis', *British Journal of Industrial Relations*, 18.

Edwards, Corwin D. (1955), 'Conglomerate Bigness as a Source of Power', in National Bureau of Economic Research conference report, *Business Concentration and Price Policy*, Princeton, N.J., Princeton University Press.

Edwards, Corwin D. (1979), 'The Multimarket Enterprise and Economic Power', *Journal of Economic Issues*, 13.

Edwards, Richard (1979), *Contested Terrain*, London, Heinemann.

Encaoua, David, Paul Geroski and Alexis Jacquemin (1983), 'Strategic Competition and the Persistence of Dominant Firms: a Survey', in F. Matthewson and J. Stiglitz (eds), *New Developments in the Analysis of Market Structure*, Cambridge, Mass., MIT Press.

Enderwick, Peter (1985), *Multinational Business and Labour*, London, Croom Helm.

Feinberg, Robert M. (1985), '"Sales-at-Risk": a Test of the Mutual Forbearance Theory of Conglomerate Behaviour', *Journal of Business*, 58.

Fellner, William J. (1949), *Competition Among the Few*, New York, Knopf.

Field, Frank (1979), *One in Eight: a Report on Britain's Poor*, Low Pay Paper No. 28, Low Pay Unit, London.

Fine, B. (1983), 'Multinational Corporations, the British Economy and the AES', *Economic Bulletin*, 10.

Forsyth, David J. C. (1972), *US Investment in Scotland*, Eastbourne, Praeger.

Friedman, Andrew L. (1977), *Industry and Labour: Class Struggle at Work and Monopoly Capitalism*, London, Macmillan.

Fröbel, Folker, Jürgen Heinrichs and Otto Kreye (1980), *The New International Division of Labour*, Cambridge, Cambridge University Press.

Gaffikin, F. and A. Nickson (1984), *Jobs Crisis and the Multinationals: Deindustrialisation in the West Midlands*, Birmingham, Third World Books.

Gaspari, K. Celeste (1983), 'Foreign Market Operations and Domestic Market Power', in Charles P. Kindleberger and David B. Audretsch (eds), *The Multinational Corporation in the 1980s*, Cambridge, Mass., MIT Press.

Gennard, John (1972), *Multinational Corporations and British Labour: A Review of Attitudes and Responses*, British-North American Committee.

Germidis, Dimitri (ed.) (1980), *International Subcontracting: a New Form of Investment*, Paris, OECD.

Ghertman, M. and M. Allen (1984), *An Introduction to Multinationals*, London, Macmillan.

Graham, E. M. (1978), 'Transatlantic Investment by Multinational Firms: a Rivalistic Phenomenon', *Journal of Post Keynesian Economics*, 1.

Greer, Charles R. and John C. Shearer (1981), 'Do Foreign-Owned US Firms Practise Unconventional Labour Relations?', *Monthly Labour Review*, 104.

Hare, Paul (1985), *Planning the British Economy*, London, Macmillan.

Helfgott, Ray B. (1983), 'American Unions and Multinational Companies: a Case of Misplaced Emphasis', *Columbia Journal of World Business*, 18.

Helleiner, Gerald K. (1981), *Intra-Firm Trade and the Developing Countries*, London, Macmillan.

Hilferding, R. (1910), *Finance Capital*, published in English in 1981, London, Routledge and Kegan.

Hirschleifer, Jack (1976), *Price Theory and Application*, London, Prentice-Hall.

Hodgson, Geoffrey (1984), *The Democratic Economy*, Harmondsworth, Penguin.

Holohan, William L. (1978), 'Cartel Problems: Comment', *American Economic Review*, 68.

Hood, Neil and Stephen Young (1979), *The Economics of Multinational Enterprise*, London, Longman.

Hymer, Stephen H. (1960), *The International Operations of National Firms*, published in 1976, Cambridge, Mass., MIT Press.

Hymer, Stephen H. (1972), 'The Multinational Corporation and the Law of Uneven Development', in J. N. Bhagwati (ed), *Economics and World Order*, London, Macmillan.

ILO (1976), *Multinationals in Western Europe: the Industrial Relations Experience*, Geneva, International Labour Office.

ILO (1976a), *Wages and Working Conditions in Multinational Enterprises*, Geneva, International Labour Office.

Imai, Ken-ichi and Hiroyuki Itami (1984), 'Interpenetration of Organisation and Market: Japan's Firm and Market in Comparison with the US', *International Journal of Industrial Organization*, 2.

Jacquemin, A. P. and N. W. de Jong (1977), *European Industrial Organisation*, London, Macmillan.

Jessop, Bob (1977), 'Recent Theories of the Capitalist State', *Cambridge Journal of Economics*, 1.

Johnson, Chalmers (1982), *MITI and the Japanese Miracle: The Growth of Industrial Policy 1925–75*, Stanford, Stanford University Press.

Johnson, C. (1985), 'Money over the Ocean', *Lloyds Bank Economic Bulletin*, October.

Kalecki, Michál (1971), *Dynamics of the Capitalist Economy*, Cambridge, Cambridge University Press.

Kamien, Morton I. and Nancy L. Schwartz (1983), 'Conjectural Variations', *Canadian Journal of Economics*, 16.

Keynes, J. M. (1982), 'National Self-Sufficiency', *New Statesman and Nation*, 1933; reprinted in D. Moggridge (ed.), *The Collected*

Writings of John Maynard Keynes, Vol. XXI, London, Macmillan.

Kilpatrick, A. and T. Lawson (1980), 'On the Nature of Industrial Decline in the UK', *Cambridge Journal of Economics*, 4.

Kindleberger, Charles P. (1969), *American Business Abroad*, New Haven, Yale University Press.

Knickerbocker, Frederick T. (1973), *Oligopolistic Reaction and Multinational Enterprises*, Boston, Harvard Business School.

Koutsoyiannis, A. (1982), *Non-Price Decisions*, London, Macmillan.

Krause, L. B. and J. S. Nye (1975), 'Reflections on the Economics and Politics of International Economic Organisation', in C. F. Bergsten and L. B. Krause (eds), *World Politics and International Economics*, Washington D.C., Brookings Institution.

Kujawa, Duane (1979), 'Collective Bargaining and Labour Relations in Multinational Enterprise: a US Public Policy Perspective', in Robert G. Hawkins (ed.), *Research in International Business and Finance*, Vol. 1, Greenwich, JAI Press.

Kujawa, Duane (1979a), 'The Labour Relations of United States Multinationals Abroad', *Labour and Society*, 4.

Lane, Tony (1982), 'The Unions: Caught on an Ebb Tide', *Marxism Today*, 26.

Lively, J. (1975), *Democracy*, Oxford, Basil Blackwell.

Macewan, Arthur (1972), 'Capitalist Expansion, Ideology, and Intervention', in Richard C. Edwards, Michael Reich and Thomas E. Weisskopf (eds), *The Capitalist System*, Englewood Cliffs, Prentice-Hall.

Machlup, F. (1967), 'Theories of the Firm: Marginalist, Behavioural, Managerial', *American Economic Review*, 57.

Mandel, Ernst (1968), *Marxist Economy Theory*, London, Merlin.

Marginson, Paul (1986), 'Labour and the Modern Corporation: Mutual Interest or Control?', *Warwick Papers in Industrial Relations*, No. 9.

Marglin, Stephen A. (1974), 'What do Bosses do?', *Review of Radical Political Economics*, 6.

Marglin, Stephen A. (1984), 'Knowledge and Power', in Frank Stephen (ed.), *Firms, Organization and Labour Approaches to the Economics of Work Organisation*, London, Macmillan.

Massey, Doreen (1984), *Spatial Divisions of Labour: Social Structures and the Geography of Production*, London, Macmillan.

McPherson, Michael (1983), 'Efficiency and Liberty in the Productive Enterprise: Recent Work in the Economics of Work Organisation', *Philosophy and Public Affairs*, 12.

Minns, Richard (1980), *Pension Funds and British Capitalism: The Ownership and Control of Shareholdings*, London, Heinemann.

Mitter, Swasti (1986), 'Industrial Restructuring and Manufacturing Homework: Immigrant Women in the UK Clothing Industry', *Capital and Class*, 27.

Monopolies Commission (1961), *Report on the Supply of Cigarettes and Tobacco and of Cigarette and Tobacco Manufacturing*, London, HMSO.

Neuberger, Henry (1985), 'Economic Planning in Britain: Comment', *Economics of Planning*, 19.

Northrup, Herbert R. (1978), 'Why Multinational Bargaining Neither Exists Nor is Desirable', *Labour Law Journal*, 29.

Osborne, Dale K. (1976), 'Cartel Problems', *American Economic Review*, 66.

Panić, M. and K. Vernon (1975), 'Major Factors behind Investment Decisions in British Manufacturing Industry', *Oxford Bulletin of Economics and Statistics*, 37.

Pateman, Carol (1970), *Participation and Democratic Theory*, Cambridge, Cambridge University Press.

Payne, R., J. Hartley and P. Warr (1983), 'Social Class and the Experience of Unemployment', Mimeo, MRR/SSRC, Social and Applied Psychology Unit, University of Sheffield.

Peretz, D. (1976), 'Finance for Investment – Issues and Non-Issues', *Banker*, April, 31.

Perry, Michael K. (1982), 'Oligopoly and Consistent Conjectural Variations', *Bell Journal of Economics*, 13.

Phillips, Almarin (1962), *Market Structure, Organisation and Performance*, Cambridge, Mass., Harvard University Press.

Pitelis, Christos N. (1982), 'Business Savings and the Macroeconomic Distribution of Income: The "Monopoly Capitalism Savings Function"', *Warwick Economic Research Papers*, 219.

Pitelis, Christos N. (1984), 'The Effects of Corporate Retentions on Personal Savings: Tests of Rival Hypotheses', AUTE/RES Conference, Bath.

Pitelis, Christos N. (1985), 'The Tendency Towards the Socialisation of the Ownership of the Means of Production and the Realisation of Profits in the Post-war UK Economy', mimeo, University of Nottingham.

Pitelis, Christos N. (1986), *Corporate Capital: Control, Ownership, Saving and Prices*, Cambridge, Cambridge University Press.

Pitelis, Christos N. and Roger Sugden (1986), 'The Separation of Ownership and Control in the Theory of the Firm: a Reappraisal', *International Journal of Industrial Organization*, 4.

Porter, Michael E. (1985), *Competitive Advantage*, New York, Free Press.

Prais, S. J. (1976), 'The Evolution of Giant Firms in Britain', Cambridge, Cambridge University Press.

Preiser, E. (1971), 'Property, Power and the Distribution of Income', in K. W. Rothschild (ed.), *Power in Economics*, London, Penguin.

Rothschild, Kurt (1942), 'A Note on Advertising', *Economic Journal*, 52.

Rugman, Alan M. (1975), 'Motives for Foreign Investment: the Market Imperfections and Risk Diversification Hypotheses', *Journal of World Trade Law*.

Rugman, Alan M. (1977), 'Risk, Direct Investment and International Diversification', *Weltwirtschaftliches Archiv*, 113.

Salop, Steven (1982), 'Practices that (Credibly) Facilitate Oligopoly Coordination', *Federal Trade Commission Bureau of Economics Working Paper*, No. 73.

Sawyer, Malcolm C. (1979), *Theories of the Firm*, London, Weidenfeld and Nicolson.

Sawyer, Malcolm C. (1981), *The Economics of Industries and Firms*, London, Croom Helm.

Scherer, F. M. (1980), *Industrial Market Structure and Economic Performance*, Chicago, Rand-McNally.

Scott, John P. (1985), *Corporations, Classes and Capitalism*, London, Hutchinson.

Scott, J. P. and M. D. Hughes (1976), 'Ownership and Control in a Satellite Economy: a Discussion from Scottish Data', *Sociology*, 10.

Scott, John T. (1982), 'Multimarket Contact and Economic Performance', *Review of Economics and Statistics*, 64.

Sharples, A. (1981), 'Alternative Economic Strategies – Labour Movement Responses to the Crisis', in D. Currie and R. Smith (eds), *Socialist Economic Review*, London, Merlin.

Sharpston, M. (1976), 'International Subcontracting', *Oxford Economic Papers*, 28.

Simon, Herbert (1959), 'Theories of Decision-Making in Economics and Behaviour Science', *American Economic Review*, 49.

Steindl, J. (1952), *Maturity and Stagnation in American Capitalism*, Oxford, Oxford University Press.

Steindl, J. (1966), 'On Maturity in Capitalist Economies', reprinted in J. B. Foster and H. Szlajfer (eds) (1984), *The Faltering Economy: The Problem of Accumulation under Monopoly Capitalism*, New York, Monthly Review Press.

Steuer, Max and John Gennard (1971), 'Industrial Relations, Labour Disputes and Labour Utilisation in Foreign-Owned Firms in the United Kingdom', in John Dunning (ed.), *The Multinational Enterprise*, London, Allen and Unwin.

Stewart, Geoff (1983), 'Workers Cooperatives and the Alternative Economic Strategy', in Malcolm Sawyer and Kerry Schott, *Socialist Economic Review*, London, Merlin.

Stoneman, P. (1983) *The Economics of Technological Change*, Oxford, Oxford University Press.

Stopford, John M. (1982), *The World Directory of Multinational Enterprises 1982–1983*, London, Macmillan.

Stopford, John M. and Louis Turner (1985), *Britain and the Multinationals*, Chichester, Wiley-IRM.

Stopford, John M., John H. Dunning and Klaus O. Haberich (1980), *The World Directory of Multinational Enterprises*, London, Macmillan.

Tomlinson, J. D. (1984), 'Economic and Sociological Theories of the Enterprise and Industrial Democracy', *British Journal of Sociology*, 35.

Ullman, Lloyd (1975), 'Multinational Unionism: Incentives, Barriers, and Alternatives', *Industrial Relations*, 14.

Ulph, David (1983), 'Rational Conjectures in the Theory of Oligopoly', *International Journal of Industrial Organization*, 1.

UNCTNC (1983), *Salient Features and Trends in Foreign Direct Investment*, New York, United Nations.

United Nations (1983), *Transnational Corporations in World Development Third Survey*, New York, United Nations.

Usher, D. (1981), *The Economic Prerequisites to Democracy*, Oxford, Basil Blackwell.

Vernon, Raymond (1966), 'International Investment and International Trade in the Product Cycle', *Quarterly Journal of Economics*, 80.

Vernon, Raymond (1972), *The Economic and Political Consequences of Multinational Enterprise: an Anthology*, Cambridge, Mass., Harvard University Press.

Vernon, Raymond (1974), 'The Location of Economic Activity', in John H. Dunning (ed.), *Economic Analysis and the Multinational Enterprise*, London, Allen and Unwin.

Vernon, Raymond (1977), *Storm Over the Multinationals*, London, Macmillan.

Vernon, Raymond (1979), 'The Product Cycle Hypothesis in a New International Environment', *Oxford Bulletin of Economics and Statistics*, 41.

Ward, T. (1981), 'The Case for an Import Control Strategy in the UK', in D. Currie and R. Smith (eds), *Socialist Economic Review*, London, Merlin.

Waterson, Michael (1984), *Economic Theory of the Industry*, Cambridge, Cambridge University Press.

Williamson, Oliver E. (1964), *The Economics of Discretionary Behavior: Managerial Objectives in a Theory of the Firm*, Engelwood Cliffs, Prentice-Hall.

Williamson, Oliver E. (1970), *Corporate Control and Business Behavior*, Englewood Cliffs, Prentice-Hall.

Williamson, Oliver E. (1975), *Markets and Hierarchies*, New York, Free Press.

Yamin, Mo (1980), 'Direct Foreign Investment as an Instrument of Corporate Rivalry: Theory and Evidence from the LDC's', *University of Manchester Department of Economics Working Paper*, No. 13.

Zeitlin, M. (1974), 'Corporate Ownership and Control: the Large Corporations and the Capitalist Class', *American Journal of Sociology*, 79.

Index